Dr. Seth's
Love
Prescription

Dr. Seth's Love Prescription

Overcome Relationship Repetition Syndrome and Find the Love You Deserve

SETH MEYERS, PsyD
with KATIE GILBERT

Introduction by #1 *New York Times* Bestselling Author Susan Forward, PhD

AVON, MASSACHUSETTS

Published by
Adams Media, a division of F+W Media, Inc.
57 Littlefield Street, Avon, MA 02322. U.S.A.
www.adamsmedia.com

ISBN 10: 1-4405-0369-9
ISBN 13: 978-1-4405-0369-6
eISBN 10: 1-4405-0914-X
eISBN 13: 978-1-4405-0914-8

Printed in the United States of America.

10 9 8 7 6 5 4 3 2 1

Library of Congress Cataloging-in-Publication Data
Meyers, Seth.
Dr. Seth's love prescription / Seth Meyers, with Katie Gilbert.
p.   cm.
Includes bibliographical references and index.
ISBN 978-1-4405-0369-6
1. Man-woman relationships. 2. Single women—Psychology. 3. Love.
I. Gilbert, Katie. II. Title.
HQ801.M547 2011
646.7'7—dc22
2010038486

The lists "Helpless Core Beliefs" and "Unlovable Core Beliefs" were previously published in *Cognitive Therapy: Basics and Beyond*, by Judith S. Beck, copyright © 1995 by Guilford Press, ISBN 10: 0-89862-847-4; ISBN 13: 978-0-89862-847-0. Reprinted with permission of The Guilford Press.

This book is available at quantity discounts for bulk purchases.
For information, please call 1-800-289-0963.

This book is dedicated to you, the reader:
May you find peace in love, and love that lasts.

Acknowledgments

I have many people to thank for their expertise, guidance, and support as I wrote this book. First, I would like to thank Dr. Susan Forward for her graciousness in having that first lunch with me, and ultimately inspiring me to put pen to paper and share my thoughts with readers. Dr. Forward's contribution is a true testament to her talent and compassion. I would also like to thank Katie Gilbert, whose insights and editing panache strengthened this book. Thanks to my editors, Paula Munier and Wendy Simard, whose careful eyes made this manuscript stronger. In addition, I want to thank my agent, Gina Panettieri, for delivering on all of her promises. Thanks to Brian, who truly taught me how to be a therapist, and to Dr. Shelley Goldklank, my graduate school mentor, who helped me understand human motivations and the complex matrix of personality. Thanks to Amanda Kane for her terrific contributions to my blog. On a more personal note, I want to thank my parents, who provided me with emotional support and wisdom throughout this process, my siblings for always making me think and laugh, and my friend JRu for helping me with my website over the years and for being an all-around good friend. Finally, I want to thank Misha, Leo, and Jonathan: I am forever grateful for what you give me.

Contents

Introduction

FOR CENTURIES, RELATIONSHIPS HAVE been the core struggle of most people's lives. It is what motivates the majority of people to seek professional help and what causes some of our deepest pain. Yet far too many people attempt to handle these struggles by repeating the same patterns that have caused pain in the past. I have seen it many hundreds of times in my thirty-five years of practice and heard it hundreds of times when I was on ABC talk radio—the old pattern of "If it doesn't work, do more of the same."

Dr. Meyers has come up with a clear and illuminating name for this pattern. He calls it "Relationship Repetition Syndrome," and he explores this multifaceted dilemma hand in hand with the reader in a no-nonsense, jargon-free style. Through examples drawn from his practice, he describes women who can't understand why their relationships never work out; who want love but continue to look for it with men who are not available for a stable, healthy relationship.

He paints a variety of vivid portraits of both actors in the drama, and provides many of the underlying causes that drive people to make self-defeating choices and repeat the same relationship behaviors as if they were hamsters on a wheel—pedaling furiously but getting nowhere.

Most important, he charts an effective route out of the maze so you can truly break the cycle of unfulfilling relationships through his "Prescription for Change," which involves insight, behavior change, and identity change. It is indeed, as he calls it, "A Winning Formula."

I know, both as a woman and as a therapist, how difficult change is for all of us—but if your relationships are one shipwreck after another, change is not only possible, but *essential*. After all, what's the alternative? We weren't born with a curse on us to be unhappy, no matter how traumatic or difficult our previous experiences have been.

You might have some hard work to do and you might get discouraged at times—being honest with yourself is never easy—but hang in there. With Dr. Meyer's compassionate guidance, you *can* find the love that you deserve.

Susan Forward, PhD
Westlake Village, California

PART I

Relationship Repetition Syndrome 101

CHAPTER 1

Relationship Repetition Syndrome

What Is It and Who Has It?

AS SOON AS MEGAN crossed the threshold into my office and closed the door behind her, I knew it had happened again: Another relationship had ended. And, as her rounded shoulders and puffy eyes made clear, she was just as devastated as last time.

She lowered herself into a chair and stared blankly out the window behind me. "Here I am again," said Megan. "I'm turning thirty next week, and all I've got to show for my twenties are about a half-dozen failed relationships." She closed her eyes. "Looking back on them now, I don't think I could even tell one from the other."

After a moment, I asked, "So what happened, Megan?"

She shook her head and pulled the sleeves of her sweatshirt over her hands. I wondered whether she was trying to warm up or draw back from my question. Finally, she said softly, "I really had myself convinced that Jay was different."

Even in her current post-breakup fog, you could easily tell that Megan was someone people were naturally drawn to and felt comfortable around. Her easy smile and big brown eyes were disarming and encouraged people to open up to her, even if they had just met her while passing through the small art gallery in downtown Los Angeles where she worked as a receptionist.

That's where she had met Jay. She didn't usually accept date invitations from men she met in the gallery, but something about Jay had excited her.

"My friends have started laughing at me when I say that—'I really think this one's different'—because they say I think that every time. But I really did think that Jay . . ." She covered her face with her hands, interrupting herself, and laughing bitterly. "Well, I won't say it again, but I *thought* he was."

"Were you right?" I asked. "Was he different?"

"No," she said, her face hardening. "He broke it off, just like they always do. I should have ended it months ago, but I stuck it out. I figured if I tried really hard to make it work, all my energy would be rewarded with this amazing relationship." She clenched her jaw and looked out the window again. "Now I'm the one with the broken heart." She paused, then looked at me. "This keeps happening to me. What am I doing wrong?"

Megan's problem was that she saw herself as helpless when it came to her own behavior. She couldn't see that she was actively seeking out the very men she later realized were bad for her. It wasn't simply happening to her—she was *making* it happen to herself. Because she hadn't stopped to look for a pattern in her string of failed relationships, she didn't realize that she had fallen prey to a compulsion, one that led her to repeatedly forge relationships with lovers who weren't right for her. Continually choosing the same type of wrong partner was as automatic and mindless for her as kicking up her leg when a doctor tapped below her knee.

A Problem of Repetition

Everyone has a relationship or two that doesn't work out, but not everyone repeatedly starts and ends relationships that so closely resemble the last failed one. This is a problem I have watched countless clients go through. These individuals are bright and energetic, and often so functional in other parts of their lives that they don't understand why they seem to be lacking in the relationship department.

As I've watched clients start new relationships while repeating the same bad patterns, I've wondered whether there is a name for this condition. I know that these women simply do the best they can with the emotional information they have, but I want to help them make sense of why their relationships never work out. I thought naming the condition could help them better understand the meaning behind their behavior.

I did a great deal of research to find whether someone had coined a term to describe this malady from which so many women and men suffer—continually repeating with the wrong types of partners. I finally concluded that what Megan and others needed was a book on why they have bad relationships and why their relationships always end.

As I thought more about the problem Megan and others suffer from, it hit me. Their problem is one of *repetition.*

If a man or woman continues to have relationships that don't work out, the relationships are failing because a toxic pattern is being repeated.

When I work with clients who continue to repeat the same bad patterns despite the unhappiness it brings them, I explain to them that repeating these patterns is akin to them banging their heads against a concrete wall. It occurred to me that I had seen a different version of this problem before. Specifically, I considered my experience working with clients who suffered from Obsessive-Compulsive Disorder (OCD). Men and women with OCD engage in compulsive behavior—behavior patterns that get stuck.

The trademark characteristic of compulsive behavior is that once sufferers start enacting a certain behavior, they have great difficulty tearing themselves away from it. They're stuck, usually repeating a behavior like hand washing, counting numbers, or checking locks. The behavior can get repeated to the extent that the sufferers cause harm to themselves. It's not unusual, for example, for people with an OCD contamination compulsion to wash their hands to the extent that their hands are covered with blisters and sores.

It occurred to me that what I see in men and women who repeat the same bad patterns in relationships is a similar concept—it's the repetition of compulsive behavior. Viewing this relationship condition as a possible quasi-relative of OCD clarifies and emphasizes the repetitive, "stuck" nature of this condition more clearly. I call this condition Relationship Repetition Syndrome (RRS).

It's important to note that RRS is not OCD. I am not suggesting that your relationship repetition indicates that you suffer from a mental disorder as outlined in the *Diagnostic and Statistical Manual of Mental Disorders*. For one thing, making such a claim would be negligent; I would need to assess you over a period of time to determine whether you have a true mental health problem.

Further, while obsession is a major component of OCD, sufferers of RRS have the opposite problem—not only are they not obsessing about the patterns of whom they choose, they're often not at all aware of them. What I am suggesting, however, is because you repeatedly find yourself in relationships with incompatible partners suggests that you sometimes engage in compulsive behavior that causes you frustration, anxiety, or a range of other negative feelings.

I believe that labeling the condition of RRS is integral in the plight to conquer it and move on. If Megan knew she had the flu, for example, she and others around her would know what to expect and how to treat it.

Women and men who suffer from RRS are what I call Relationship Repeaters, or RRs. There are four dysfunctional, repeated patterns—idealizing the external, emotional chasing, rescuing wounded souls, and sacrificing yourself—that characterize RRS. Women of all ages, backgrounds, and levels of intelligence can repeat one or more of these four toxic patterns, which we'll review in the upcoming chapters.

What Is RRS?

RRS is a vicious behavioral cycle in which you:

- Repeat at least one of four patterns that sabotage your romantic relationships: You either idealize partners based on external characteristics, sacrifice yourself, try to save wounded souls, or emotionally chase your partners
- Find yourself attracted to partners who don't meet your emotional needs
- Find yourself attracted to the same characteristics that ultimately make you unhappy in your relationships
- Prioritize the wrong characteristics as you seek out partners
- Struggle to find a partner who truly understands or "gets" you
- Consistently realize belatedly that your partner is not the right one for you

RRS can show up in all types of relationships. You can find yourself repeating the same toxic patterns and ending up with the wrong person in any of the following stages of a relationship:

- Dating
- Short-term relationships
- Long-term relationships
- Marriages

You may balk at the idea that someone can repeat toxic patterns in marriage, because we tend to think of marriage as lasting a lifetime. Yet consider that the divorce rate is approximately 50 percent and that many divorced men and women later remarry and divorce again. Think for a minute about those who have *multiple* marriages. I'm guessing not only can you think of celebrities who continue to get married and divorced, but you can probably also think of someone in your personal life who's gone through that.

The Difference Between Relationship Repeaters and Healthy Lovers

Let's face it: Relationships can be difficult for everyone. As the saying goes, "You have to kiss a lot of frogs to catch a prince." Most people have had a relationship or two that didn't work out. What separates healthy lovers from women and men with RRS is the degree of repetition and suffering. RRs feel caught in a cycle in which they cannot get off the bad relationship merry-go-round. Their relationships end, and yet again and again they seek out the same type of partner they swore off after their last painful breakup. They repeat the same mistakes because they have been unable to glean emotional lessons from their past relationships and learn from them. On the other hand, healthy lovers try to avoid what didn't work the last time—they aren't stuck. Instead, they propel themselves forward toward something new and different to avoid the hurt and pain of their last failed relationship.

SELF-EVALUATION
Take Inventory of Your Relationship History

1. Do you feel like you are only sexually attracted to partners who are bad for you?

2. Have you found yourself in a relationship with someone who does the same kinds of things your last significant other did that hurt or bothered you?

3. Do your friends and families comment on your choosing the wrong partners and ask why you haven't settled down with the right person?

4. Do your relationships tend to last a certain amount of time and then consistently end after the same approximate length of time? For example, perhaps you've never made it past the three-year hurdle.

5. Have you ever fallen for someone by simply looking at him or watching him, or decided you want to be with him within the first few minutes of meeting?

6. Do you find yourself feeling the same kinds of negative feelings you felt in your last relationship, precipitated by the same kinds of situations?

7. Do you blame yourself or your partners for why things went wrong?

8. Do you sometimes feel like you lose yourself in your relationships?

9. Do you feel like you are cursed to have bad relationships and will never find "The One"?

If you answered "yes" to two or more of these questions, you suffer from RRS. If you answered "yes" to one of the questions, you suffer from some of the symptoms of RRS.

This book will ask you to work through a comprehensive program to break the cycle of RRS. You will use this simple model to apply my program:

Insight + Behavior Change = Identity Change

Once we can modify the way you have relationships and see yourself in them, you can move on to live a happy life and find a partner you're compatible with. You will do your own inventories in the major areas of your life, begin a program of new behaviors, and then be asked to apply what you've learned. By following my program, you will break the cycle of RRS.

I have spent many years undergoing training to treat clients with relationship problems. In my practice and at various clinics, I have provided individual and group therapy to countless individuals who suffered in their relationships. I wrote this book with the intention to give you the "Greatest Hits" of my clinical experience. In this book I borrow from all the disciplines I have had access to in my professional experience, including psychoanalytic theory, cognitive-behavioral theories, and the Alcoholics Anonymous Twelve-Step model. This book will offer you:

- A breakthrough theory of why you repeat bad patterns (it's not always because of your childhood or a lack of self-esteem)
- A foolproof method of approaching your existing relationship or creating a new one
- Coping skills and strategies to prevent "relationship relapse"
- Tools that will equip you to ask your partners the right questions in the beginning, so that you invest in a solid relationship
- A groundbreaking behavioral strategy that asks you to engage in uncomfortable but necessary behaviors to stop repeating the four dysfunctional relationship patterns

While the first part outlines each of the four patterns, the second and third parts focus on the model for change and hands-on insight inventories. Finally, the fourth and fifth parts focus on behaviors that will help you reshape the way you approach relationships so that you can move on and put an end to your suffering in relationships. By the time you finish my program, you will be more conscious of your behavior in your relationships so that someday you may find yourself sitting across the dinner table from someone who's right for you!

How to Use this Book

You will need a notebook, and a computer will help, too. When I discuss concepts that interest you, you can search online for more information. Ideally, this book should be used as a primer to get you started on your journey toward creating a new relationship identity.

Some of the things I will ask you to do while you work through the program might make you feel uncomfortable. However, this discomfort is necessary for you to change. To signify difficult exercises, I call them "Hot Coals Tasks." They will be called out with a special icon: 🔥. The idea is that you must get through them to develop stronger, thicker skin. I use all of these techniques regularly in my clinical practice and have watched them literally transform many women's lives for the better.

What is the number one tool to take with you along your journey? Curiosity. Be curious about why you have chosen the partners you have, and be curious about why you may have stayed longer than you should have. Use the frustration and sadness you feel because your relationship dream hasn't yet come true, and channel it into figuring out *why*. Once you know why, you will be better armed to activate the best part of yourself. You truly *can* change certain behaviors and you *can* learn to become attracted to partners with whom you're more emotionally compatible. With the help of this book, you can solidify a new, healthier relationship identity. Soon you will say to yourself, "Yes, I can and will find love that lasts."

CHAPTER 2

Pattern #1

Idealizing the External

VALERIE CAME TO SEE me in the early spring, explaining that "the thought of another summer full of other people's weddings has driven me to therapy." However, after we got past our initial introductory chat, I gathered that Valerie's recent breakup with a man named Steve also had something to do with her decision to visit my office.

Valerie played with her necklace as she told me that she was pleased, for the most part, with the way life had arranged itself around her. She liked her job in the administrative office of the large university she'd attended as an undergraduate, she owned her own townhouse, and had just gotten a puppy. She remained close with her best friends from college, most of whom had stayed in Los Angeles, as she had.

"I should have everything I need to be happy," she said. The way her voice caught on that last word suggested she was trying to convince herself that this was the case.

As she'd entered her late twenties, she watched her friends steadily pair off into serious relationships and marriages. She became desperate about a pattern in her life that had only nagged at her before: None of her relationships ever made it past the six-month hurdle. Though she described herself as a "die-hard romantic" and dated constantly, nothing seemed to stick.

She had met Steve the previous autumn at an alumni barbeque before her alma mater's homecoming football game. She hadn't known him well in college—he was two years older than she—but she'd certainly noticed him.

"Steve has always been absolutely gorgeous, someone who gives people whiplash when he walks into a room," Valerie said. "He's got it all—he's tall, with broad shoulders, a chiseled jaw, this big white smile. I could never work up enough courage to talk to him in college, but things have changed. I've changed. I've dated some pretty good-looking guys since then, which has done wonders for my confidence."

They spent the rest of the alumni event by one another's side. Valerie glowed as she remembered how good it felt for all of her college classmates to see her sitting next to—and then holding hands with—Steve.

Things moved quickly, and within weeks Valerie thought of their relationship as serious. She wanted to be with him all the time. His presence gave her that same high no matter where they were—sitting in restaurants, walking on the sidewalk, or even meandering through the grocery store. She could tell that everyone around them was noting what a beauty she'd landed by the way they stared.

"I fell hard for him right away," Valerie recalled. "But after only two months or so I noticed things starting to . . . fizzle. I remember one weekend we took a trip up the coast. It was all planned to perfection—the bed-and-breakfast, the candlelit dinners, the tour of wine country—and it just flopped. I haven't told anyone this, but I was so relieved when it was over and I got home." She shook her head as she remembered the weekend's awkwardness.

"You know on the drive up there, we were silent and staring out the window more than we were talking? And I'm a notorious talker! I'd comment on something out the window—a funny billboard or a car with a dragon painted on the side—and he'd just purse his lips and nod, like he didn't get it. I realized then that we just didn't get a kick out of the same things. Eventually I just gave up." But Valerie didn't totally give up after that weekend—she still had grand plans for the relationship and badly wanted it to last. It wasn't until several months later that the relationship petered out completely.

A Fixed Image

Idealizing external characteristics failed Valerie because she became bored and unfulfilled. I could also see that repeating this pattern had an additional psychological effect on her: Continually ending relationships left her feeling depressed. The gloominess revealed itself in several symptoms. She had little interest in socializing with her friends anymore, which had been one of her favorite ways to spend time. She also started to feel hopeless about the prospect of a relationship that would last.

Valerie started to realize that it was going to take longer than she'd planned to find a partner. Many of her girlfriends from college had started families, and she hoped to do the same. She had daydreamed that she and her girlfriends would raise their kids at the same time and swap stories and offer support to each other, but she realized that she was already falling behind them.

Valerie fell prey to the illusion that the physical attractiveness of a man could be enough to fulfill her, but she wasn't considering what she needed emotionally. She was not aware that she put a greater priority on sexual and physical attraction than on emotional compatibility.

As she did with Steve, Valerie routinely found herself putting all of her energy into realizing her fantasy of being with someone physically attractive and neglected to seek out a strong emotional bond with the men she pursued. While healthy lovers become more flexible about their "type" as they get older, she held on to this fixed image and routinely sought out the same type of man.

Idealizing Appearance Never Works

Valerie felt bored and alone in her relationship, and she's in good company: countless other women fall for partners based on external characteristics and end up disappointed by their emotional incompatibility. Valerie's dream of finding lasting love died because she idealized characteristics that did not ultimately make her happy.

Idealizers repeatedly seek out partners with specific external characteristics because they believe that these surface features will be enough to fulfill them in the relationship. Some women may make finding attractive men their number one priority. Other women's attractiveness priority may be more age-related. These women may seek out older, sophisticated-looking men, or perhaps younger trophy boyfriends. Don't be misled: Men aren't the only ones in today's society looking for a trophy to adorn them!

THE IDEALIZER:

- Is drawn to partners with a particular physical type, appearance, professional status (whether it's a great job or no job at all), level of ambition, or age, and prioritizes those external characteristics above all else.
- Often places more importance on sexual attractiveness than emotional attractiveness (which could be evidenced by kindness, strong communication skills, a shared world view, and strong relationships with family and friends).
- Often sees her partner as a reflection of herself, and wants to convey the image her partner represents.
- Harbors the fantasy that someone with the appearance or professional status she is drawn to will be enough to make her happy.
- Typically feels like she has little in common with her partner by the end of the relationship.

Having an attractive partner serves as a validation, which RRs often require to offset their own insecurities. These RRs feel that their partners are their extensions and that they can project a more attractive, sophisticated, or younger version of themselves by having the right type of partner on their arm. The priority for RRs who idealize in this way is to find partners who meet their appearance criteria.

They do not place sufficient priority on their partners' internal characteristics, including their values, their ability to communicate, and their openness to intimacy.

Even if the RRs see faults in their partners, they are often willing to overlook them as long as their partners meet the guidelines of their all-important appearance checklist.

A Variation on the Theme: Patricia's Story

On the surface, what holds Valerie back in her relationships appears different from what holds back my friend Patricia. But the two women's problems spring from the same source.

For years, I have watched as Patricia soldiers through relationships that don't work out. She is intent on meeting a certain type of man, and frequently succeeds: She only dates successful businessmen. She is attracted to men with great ambition, and immediately after meeting them begins fantasizing about the kind of life they'll have together.

Patricia also talks openly about how having nice things is very important to her because she grew up with very little. She came from a tiny Midwestern town that had one small school, a few stoplights, and a ramshackle general store. When she was young, she made a pact with herself to someday leave all that behind and make a life for herself someplace far away and glamorous. She managed to make good on that promise to herself, and has a job as a saleswoman at a makeup counter in a high-end department store.

Behind the makeup counter, with her cool green eyes and sharp cheekbones, she looks like one of the statuesque models pictured in the posters that surround her and attracts attention from the types of men whom, as a child, she always imagined filled the big cities—suit-donning, sophisticated-looking men who practically smelled like success.

Although she always ends up with well-off men, she insists that she doesn't intentionally seek them out. She argues that they simply "happen to" have money. Patricia considers herself old-fashioned in that she likes a man to hold the door for her and to take her out for nice dinners. She looks for a man to provide for her financially, and she believes that she brings other qualities to the table.

As I watched Patricia go through her last relationship, I found that it had the same doomed patterns of all her other failed relationships. After Patricia had been with Sam for about a year, the relationship began to grate on both of them. They fought frequently and seemed to misunderstand each other during arguments. Sam felt that Patricia took advantage of him and was overly demanding, while Patricia felt that Sam did not appreciate her and rarely made the types of elaborate gestures—buying jewelry, surprising her with flowers, whisking her off on weekend getaways—that people in love are supposed to make.

Soon Patricia was angry all the time. She was angry at Sam for not appreciating her enough. She was angry because she thought she had finally found a strong man to provide for her, and her dream was not unfolding according to her plan. By the end of the relationship, Patricia's anger got the best of her, and she broke up with Sam during an explosive argument.

"Some of the things he said to me during that last fight still ring in my ears," Patricia said, shaking her head as if trying to loosen the memories from her mind. "He called me manipulative and—worse—a gold digger. I couldn't believe someone could see me like that. I told him I never wanted to see him again." She exhaled slowly. "And I haven't."

What continued to drive Patricia crazy is that she couldn't pinpoint exactly where things went wrong.

"In the beginning, he seemed to be fine with our setup—he certainly loved the sex with me. But later, he started pulling this drama about how I expect too much from him. One time, when we were buying a gift for my friend's birthday, he took it out of my hands and said

"I guess it's my job to pay for that, right?" It came out of nowhere—he usually just paid for things and was fine with it! When did he start getting bothered by that? He makes a lot of money and I'm an old-fashioned girl. Is it too much for me to like a man to treat me well?"

As Patricia talked about their arguments, the resentment in the room grew palpable and clearly encompassed much more than Sam. She had fallen for the same kind of man over and over, and had accumulated a massive load of anger because she was always unhappy in the end. There was too wide a gulf between Patricia and her boyfriends, and somehow each person ended up feeling misunderstood.

The External at Odds with the Emotional

The problem for Patricia was that she idealized an external characteristic—her boyfriend's professional status—in the belief that he could provide a certain lifestyle for her. In the end, however, the relationships ended up taking a toll on Patricia. Idealizing her partner's professional status set her back developmentally, because she spent a great deal of time investing in relationships that never went anywhere. In healthy relationships, the shared foundation and chemistry between two partners brings out the best in both. The relationship helps each partner grow and move forward. In Patricia's case, repeating this idealizing pattern had delayed her emotional maturity.

Because Patricia's relationships did not last long, she did not go through the difficult milestones inherent in a long-term relationship. Switching relationships so often and not committing to a lasting one meant that she never had to sit with someone through the difficult but normal cycles in a long-term relationship. Because these rough patches in a lasting relationship yield some of the most meaningful growth, Patricia had missed a fundamental step in the progression toward the wisdom and acceptance of reality that, hopefully, comes with adulthood.

Patricia often wanted to end her relationships when things got difficult, and she became impatient when she saw aspects of her partner that she didn't like. She had great difficulty exploring her own uncomfortable feelings and accepting realities that were not to her liking.

Idealizing Professional Status Also Never Works

Patricia felt angry and frustrated in her relationship with Sam because she felt cheated. But the problem was her own: She didn't think at all about her emotional needs in the process of seeking out partners. Just as Valerie prioritized the appearance of her boyfriend rather than focusing on what characteristics would meet her emotional needs and fulfill her, Patricia prioritized her boyfriend's professional status with the same result. Neither woman placed a sufficient priority on the characteristics that build a strong emotional foundation and fortify a relationship to become meaningful and lasting.

Patricia was drawn to Sam because she thought his ambition and professional status meant that he was strong and could provide a comfortable lifestyle for her, but she learned they had little in common. Though Sam was financially successful, she did not place equal importance on how emotionally successful he was. She never considered the quality of his friendships, his relationships with his family members, and his interests outside of work. In addition, she failed to give equal consideration to how well he communicated with her, how kind he was, and how emotionally mature he was. These factors are important indicators of what kind of partner a man will be, but Patricia fell into a trap wherein she idealized Sam and the other men she dated based solely on their professional status and financial position.

Like many women, Patricia was not aware that she was doing this—she truly didn't realize what a one-track mind she'd developed in her search for the right partner. After all, it is easier for us to be objective with others than it is to be so with ourselves. What was obvious to others simply wasn't to her. She wasn't shallow or overly dependent, but she did have some work to do. She needed to learn to give up idealistic fantasies in favor of making good decisions that draw upon the kind of wise judgment that comes from learning from bad experiences.

At this point it should be said that there is nothing wrong with seeking out partners who are financially successful as long as you place equal—or greater—importance on other internal factors. The goal is to look at all the characteristics of your potential partners, and not prioritize an external characteristic to determine whether the mix is a good match for you. If you see a pattern in which your relationships continue to end, it means that it's time to take a closer look at what ingredients you're putting into your relationship recipe.

Does This Sound Like You?

There is more than one version of this repetitive pattern. While Patricia was an example of an RR who repeated the pattern with financially successful men, others may seek out other types of partners based on a different type of professional status. Other RRs may seek out individuals with a certain kind of career, perhaps one that is associated with an unconventional lifestyle. This could include attraction to dancers, artists, or musicians. It could also include falling for a workaholic.

Another version of this type may surprise you: Some RRs who repeat the pattern based on professional status may actually seek out individuals who have no job, a go-nowhere job, or who have little or no ambition and are looking for a free ride. RRs who seek out this type of individual may do so for many reasons. When RRs are financially successful themselves, they sometimes believe that they will be more needed or have more power in their relationships with such individuals. For those RRs who are not financially successful either, they may seek out such individuals because they feel intimidated by those who are successful.

What do all of the RRs share in common? They share the fact that seeking out the same type of partner continues to result in failed relationships. Even though the RRs are repeatedly drawn and attracted to partners based on some idealized external characteristic or trait, once they are in the relationship they are faced with the same unfulfilling or frustrating characteristics that have ended all of their previous relationships.

THE TAKEAWAY

As you can see from Valerie's and Patricia's stories, the relationships of idealizers consistently end because they don't place a sufficient priority on the internal, emotional characteristics of their partners. In their quest to find partners who meet their specific desired physical characteristic or professional status checklist, they neglect their emotional needs and avoid the reality that there must be good *emotional* chemistry for a relationship to be healthy and long-lasting. Those who idealize external characteristics mistakenly tell themselves that meeting this criterion is enough to fulfill them, and they don't think about the factors two people really need to make it through thick and thin. RRs who idealize external characteristics must exchange their idealistic fantasies for real-world, adult realities and expectations in order to create a positive, lasting union. In Part II, you'll learn how to train your focus on more important traits.

SELF-EVALUATION
The External Versus the Emotional

1. How would someone describe your professional and physical type? Write down these external characteristics.

2. Has anyone ever idealized any of your external characteristics? Did you feel truly appreciated by these suitors?

3. Why do you think it's tempting to idealize external characteristics?

4. Can you think of people you know who repeat this pattern?

5. What are some emotional attributes that are worthy of more attention in the beginning of a relationship? Write them down and keep this list for later.

CHAPTER 3

Pattern #2

Emotional Chasing

WHEN I FIRST SAW Daphne, she looked like she'd walked out of a black-and-white movie. Her dark hair in a sleek bob, her bright red lipstick, and her black dress exuded a casual elegance. So it came as little surprise to me when she admitted her weakness for old movies, especially love stories. She loved watching the dramatic turnaround, where at the beginning of the movie, the leading man is a wanderer who can't be tied down, and by the end, the leading woman has won him over and brought out the lovesick inner husband in him.

When I asked Daphne why she'd come to see me, she explained simply that she was getting nowhere in love. Not only was she thirty-seven and unmarried—she'd been planning her wedding and had names picked out for her children since before she could remember—but none of her relationships, some of which lasted several years, had even came close to marriage territory. Recently, her best friend had pointed out a pattern about Daphne that she wanted to further explore with me: Daphne tended to stay with partners—sometimes for a very long time—who were never as committed to their relationship as she was.

One boyfriend, a graphic designer named Alex, had smiled and emphatically agreed to move in together when she'd suggested it was time. But the move-in date was delayed into perpetuity by excuses:

questions about how they'd fit all their furniture into the same small-ish apartment, and, eventually, discussions about his fear that living with her would keep him from getting work done in his home office. Even after they agreed to table the move-in plans, she'd stayed with him for another two years.

"I know, I know," Daphne said, shaking her head and laughing. "From where I sit now, it's obvious that our relationship was never going to end well. He was never going to commit. But that whole time, I was just so sure that one day he'd see the light and realize how lucky he was to have me," she said. "Suffice it to say he never did."

Another of her multiyear relationships had been with a man named Mitch. From their first date, he'd been very clear: She wasn't the only one. He wanted to keep seeing her, but just so she knew, he wasn't seeing her exclusively. She always told him nonchalantly that she was fine with the setup.

"I wasn't fine with the setup," she told me, her voice rising. "Of course I wasn't! Especially after we'd been together for two and a half years, I was most definitely not fine with the setup. But something in me needed to know that I could win him over, to prove to myself that I could make him want to be with just me."

"Why do you think you needed to know that?" I asked.

She took a deep breath and sat up a little straighter. "Maybe it's the competitive gymnast in me," she said with a half smile. "I like to win."

"So it wasn't about Mitch by the end—it was about the pursuit?"

"To be honest, I'm not even sure it was about Mitch at the beginning."

Without realizing it, Daphne attached herself to men who she sensed wouldn't easily commit. This type of man gave her just enough love and attention for her to get a taste of what she wanted. But instead of saying *this isn't enough* and walking away, she would attempt to tame him and show Mr. Unavailable the she was the one worth settling down for.

In the process, she wasn't doing herself any favors. The types of men she chased were bound to move on eventually, regardless of who Daphne was or what she did. As she desperately continued trying to blot out past rejections with a romantic win, she merely accumulated more and more rejections.

Chasing Secretive Partners

Unlike Daphne, Candice had once been very close to marriage—so close that her dress had been fitted, invitations had gone out, and the reception hall had been booked. But a month and a half before the big day, her fiancé, Ken, who had been her boyfriend for six years, since they were freshmen in high school, tearfully told her that he couldn't go through with it. She was stunned to hear that he'd secretly been cheating on her for a year. Immediately after his admission, the wedding was called off. Although she said she'd told the story dozens of times, tears streamed down Candice's face once more as she recounted the memory during our first session.

Candice said that about a year and a half after the breakup, she'd suddenly felt ready to "wade into the sea, finally meet a few new fish." But re-entering the dating world didn't end up being the quick pick-me-up her friends and family assured her it would be. Either she felt absolutely no spark with the men she met through online dating services and blind dates, or they eventually turned out to be just as secretive as Ken had been.

"You'd think after having my heart ripped to shreds once before, I'd know all the signs of a potential cheater and avoid him like the plague," Candice said. "But no. It's like I'm a magnet to these guys. Do I have a sign on my forehead that says, 'Cheaters, please apply here?'"

Candice felt like she'd spent the whole three years since she and Ken broke up dating cheater after cheater, but in fact she'd only been cheated on by two men since she'd had to cancel her near-marriage. A just-as-significant part of the problem, and the reason that so much of her time had been eaten up by these types of boyfriends, was that she stayed with men long after she saw the unavoidable signs of their philandering. They'd keep shadowy portions of their social lives secret from her, come home late after a night of "hanging with the guys" and not make eye contact when they granted vague details of the night. It only made matters worse to socialize with them when she began to predict her ability to follow their gaze at parties and watch it linger a beat too long on attractive women.

"I admit that each time, I come to a point where I know what's going on. I always know when I'm being cheated on again," Candice said as she looked down. "But for some reason, in the moment that's all the more reason to stay. I tell myself 'I can stick this out, he'll see that I'm the one sticking by his side and figure out that I'm the one he really wants.'"

Candice wasn't crazy or delusional, nor suspicious or distrusting by nature. She wasn't hell-bent on believing that her partners were doing something to betray her. The reality was that, like Daphne, she was compulsively trying to tame something in her partners that was not ready to be tamed. To add insult to injury, she took their unavailability personally. Candice's youth and inexperience in the relationship arena contributed to these misguided beliefs. Since she'd been in the same relationship since high school, she hadn't had the chance to have dating experiences with men that could have taught her important life lessons.

The Dangers of Putting Your Partner on a Pedestal

The first time Terry came into my office, she lowered her tall frame onto the couch, ran her fingers through her hair, and dove right in: "Something's wrong with the way I think about relationships. I just don't know quite what," she said. As Terry explained it, she had some-how become "romantically blocked." After talking with her a bit more, I learned that Terry was prone to putting her partners on pedestals.

"I'm thirty-eight, and I've had three serious relationships—a tiny fraction of the number most people my age have had. I don't get it."

It wasn't for lack of options. She regularly had male friends, acquaintances, and strangers express interest in dating her, but she'd grown deft in the art of letting them down softly. With very, very few exceptions, she just wasn't interested. Friends teased her about being picky to a fault, yet Terry didn't think that was it. She didn't have a particular type she was keeping her eye out for, she just wanted to feel a spark. A few sessions later, though, she did reveal that it was a real turnoff when she met a man who seemed "too" interested in her. A man had to give off a little mystery, she said.

I asked her to walk me through her dating history and she told me about Eliot, the green-eyed boy who had been her first love.

Eliot and Terry had been best friends throughout high school, and she had fallen deeply in love with him. But the friendship with Eliot never grew into anything more. While other young men expressed interest, Terry had set her sights on Eliot and fervently believed he was the one and only boy for her. She'd lost touch with him after occasionally corresponding during college, but still, after all these years, found herself thinking about him when she went to weddings, or watched a romantic movie, or read an article about whether soul mates really existed. She'd never completely been able to get Eliot out of her system.

Yet her fixation on Eliot had waned with time, especially when she'd met Patrick a few years ago. That relationship had started out like a fantasy for her: She was dining alone at a dark, ritzy restaurant one night when a man approached her and said that his friend, Patrick, would like to say hello. When she turned around in her booth and saw him, Terry couldn't believe that Patrick wanted to meet her. He looked like a chiseled Cary Grant under the single light bulb that hung over his booth. Her heart leapt when she noticed him staring at her. She'd never seen anything like him.

She moved over to Patrick's booth and was instantly mesmerized by the calm, cool, restrained way he interacted with her and his friends. Terry especially liked how confident he appeared and was further turned on as she saw other women gazing at him from across the room.

The relationship with Patrick was intense from the beginning. She worked hard to impress him and tried not to let a minute pass—whether they were together or not—when she wasn't doing something to earn, secure, and ensure his love. She left notes all over his apartment, surprised him with tickets to exclusive events, and mastered a gourmet risotto dish—his favorite meal. But with the intensity that Terry was purposefully keeping up came a constant, dull panic; how could she keep one-upping herself, let alone maintain the romance? She asked her friends for ideas, but she never felt that she did enough. Terry wanted more than anything to ensure that she could keep Patrick. A man like that, she told herself, could fly away at any moment without a second thought.

After several months of trying to do everything she could to impress him and keep him interested, Terry found herself feeling increasingly anxious. She never felt certain as to whether he liked the activities she chose, and she sometimes spent money beyond her budget on things she hoped he'd like. About ten months into the relationship, she took a friend's advice and decided to stop trying so hard, to just be herself and let the relationship unfold naturally. Blind-sided by the 180, Patrick told her he could tell she was losing interest and that he was moving on. It was just as well—Terry was broke and exhausted.

The Thrill of the Chase

In her relationship with Patrick and her affection for Eliot, Terry got stuck emotionally chasing men she put on a pedestal. She viewed them as one-in-a-million catches who could have any woman they wanted.

Of course, healthy lovers are excited to land a great catch, too. But RRs who repeat this pattern are thrown into a state of sheer bliss in their belief that they have found the most special person ever. They feel renewed, validated, invincible. They see their dates or lovers as one in a billion, often from the moment they meet.

RRs who emotionally chase their partners by putting them on a pedestal tend to be dreamers. They are people who indulge in dramatic expressions of love. They adore grand gestures, including surprise trips and rooms filled with huge bouquets of flowers. They have a hard time imagining themselves settling for a love that is anything less than romantic and intense.

But by catapulting Patrick to an exalted status, Terry had lowered herself as less-than. At root, she questioned why someone of his caliber would have any interest in her. When I asked her whether she had a low impression of herself, she made a joke and dismissed the question. However, if Terry truly considered herself to be a great catch, she would expect a world-class knockout to be interested in her—she wouldn't be surprised.

The truth is that, deep down, RRs who repeat the pattern of putting their partners on a pedestal see their partners as too good for them, better than they are themselves, or unattainable. People like Terry are turned on by the chase and, sadly, by their partner's emotional unavailability. What motivates them is the prospect that if they can attain the love and affection of the lovers up on that pedestal—the ultimate type of love, as they see it—they can finally experience the bliss of feeling good enough.

THE EMOTIONAL CHASER:

- Tends to have partners who ultimately won't commit and settle down, who cheat on her, or whom she puts on a pedestal.
- Is usually more emotionally committed to her relationship than her partner is.
- Feels like her partner has all the control and power in the relationship.
- Often feels less worthy than her partner, as if her partner were more interesting or desirable.
- Believes she has to work hard to keep him interested because she feels that he could very easily slide through her fingers and slip away.
- Tries to shape herself into being what she thinks her partner wants.

- Notices that her partners always seem to have excuses for why they can't make more time for her or why they don't want to take the relationship to the next level.
- Feels like she's waiting and hoping for her partner to realize that she's the one he really wants.

THE TAKEAWAY

Daphne, Candice, Terry, and other emotional chasers have all made a common inner vow, often unbeknownst to them: They're going to prove to unavailable partners that they *are* good enough, that they *are* worth settling down for. Terry suffered as a result of emotionally chasing men she put on a pedestal. She was not unlike Daphne and Candice, who chased men who either wouldn't commit or who engaged in secretive behavior that resulted in betrayal. Though their partners look different on the surface, RRs who emotionally chase their partners all share the same drive: They are on a mission to win the love of unavailable partners. Whether you emotionally chase someone who won't commit, someone who is secretive, or someone you put on a pedestal, the fact is that you're playing a losing game.

SELF-EVALUATION
Deconstructing the Chase

1. Who in your life have you emotionally chased? In other words, whose affection and love you have worked hard to get but have never fully received? Which kind of emotional chasing did you engage in?

2. How did the chase end? Did you get what you wanted?

3. What was the most difficult part of the situation to accept?

4. Looking back, was the chasing done in pursuit of a specific person, or did it become about something bigger?

CHAPTER 4

Pattern #3

Rescuing Wounded Souls

I FIRST MET MEGAN—the RR from Chapter 1—at a conference, just after I had finished giving a talk about how to start your own private practice. She approached me, gingerly inquiring as to whether she might be able to meet with me in my practice. She looked exhausted and I didn't want her to have to wait too long, so we decided to meet for our first session that same week.

At first, we spent most of our time talking about her childhood. She described it as "good enough, as childhoods go, with a few blips here and there," and I gathered that most of those blips had occurred in the gaps between her alcoholic father's intermittent periods of sobriety. When he was sober, he was a doting and involved father, but when he drank, his temper was hot enough to set the house on fire. Megan recalled many nights during his absence or during his yelling rampages when she'd take her younger sister's hand, tiptoe into their mother's room, and do whatever she could—tell jokes or stories from her day, ask her mother to read aloud—to distract them from crying. Somehow she had come to feel responsible and wanted to make sure everyone else was okay.

It was when we started talking about her romantic relationships that I understood why she'd sought counseling. As she approached thirty, she'd been reflecting on her twenties and the ways in which she'd changed and matured over the course of the decade. As she evaluated each part of her life, she realized with stark clarity that one thing hadn't changed at all: She was still struggling through the same types of problems in her relationships as she had been since she was much younger.

To illustrate what had become the stubborn blueprint of her romantic life, she told me about her most recent breakup, with Jay. She'd fallen hard almost instantaneously when he first came into the gallery where she worked. As she followed his thoughtful drifting between paintings, she found herself intrigued by how mysterious and brooding he seemed.

Jay came into the gallery several times over the next few weeks, and eventually he and Megan began to chat. He was perceptibly nervous when they first started talking, which Megan found charming, and he had a sweet, boyish smile that he flashed often and that made Megan's heart contract in her chest. He wrote short fiction and asked if she'd like to go to a reading with him at a bookstore nearby. She gladly accepted.

You can probably guess that more dates followed. More than anything, Megan loved walking and talking with Jay. When she was with him, she could tell she was in the presence of a fascinating mind and that he was on the brink of something big with his writing. She encouraged him in his work and told him how great she believed his potential to be. He seemed heartened by her praise, and Megan believed it was a sign that they were getting serious when he began to open up to her about his bouts of depression and anxiety attacks. Sometimes in his candid chats with Megan, she sensed that he was almost trying to warn her. He told her that his past girlfriends had accused him of having a commitment phobia, and added, with resignation, that they were probably right. Megan would take his hand and squeeze it, and tell him how much she cared about him. Though he never acknowledged it outright, Megan knew that she was a solid, steadying presence that he badly needed in his life.

"I knew he wasn't perfect, and I knew it wasn't a perfect relationship," she said. "But I'm not perfect either, and besides, I'm not looking for perfect. Isn't love about seeing someone for who they could be, not who they are, cheesy as it sounds?" Megan paused, then continued, "Isn't love about never giving up on someone?"

Megan euphemistically framed their relationship as not quite perfect, but her friends were more blunt: They told her that the relationship had become a massive burden on her. After Megan and Jay had been together for a few months, he started regularly showing up late to pick her up for dates, and sometimes he was so distant or snappish when they were together that she wished he hadn't come to pick her up at all. Even more troubling to Megan was the fact that he never talked about a future with her. Megan recalled getting angry when he accused her of "trying to force the relationship into high gear" when she suggested he come to her mom's house for Thanksgiving.

"What are *you* getting out of this?" and "What's it going to take for you to end it?" became questions she heard incessantly from her friends. She'd tell them that they didn't know Jay the way she did, that they had no firsthand knowledge of how talented he was, and that they had no idea just how much in common they had. Megan felt an irreplaceable connection with Jay as they walked through museums and galleries, hand in hand, talking about art and whatever else popped into their minds. Megan also saw what her friends couldn't—that he wanted to change, to be better for her. Whenever he'd snap, or not show up as her date at a gallery event he'd said he would attend, he was genuinely and effusively apologetic the next day. In those moments, he would get down on himself and tell Megan she didn't deserve to be with someone who acted like he did. Without fail, she trusted his good intentions, and reminded herself to be patient with him.

On a couple of occasions when Megan's patience had expired, she tried to end the relationship. Each time, her voice had faltered as she tried to tell him what she had to do, and each time, he saw what was coming and started to cry. Guilt overcame her, and in each of those moments one thought took front and center in her mind: Jay was a nice man who didn't deserve to be broken up with or abandoned. Given time, she could help him overcome his neuroses and his inability to commit. Patience would eventually produce in him the man of her dreams, she figured—never mind that that method had never worked her previous boyfriends.

"But he left," she told me. "He just got in his car and drove away, and told me not to follow him." She fell silent for a moment. "When my last boyfriend left me, I remember telling a friend that it was like I'd been scammed: I tried to leave, but he begged me not to, only to turn around and leave me. And look, now the same exact thing has happened." Her eyes welled. "Will I ever learn not to fall for this again?"

Why a "Fix-It" Attitude Backfires

Though the names and faces of the men Megan dated changed, something more crucial did not: All of her boyfriends were wounded souls who carried tremendous emotional baggage. Invariably, she failed to see exactly how unhealthy these men were until it was too late, and by that point she had already fallen in love with them. As I worked initially with Megan, I began to get a better sense of the pattern she repeated. It was unlike emotional chasing, the pattern we discussed in Chapter 3; Megan's relationship problems were due to something different. While men who are emotionally chased truly don't want to settle down and find true intimacy, men who are wounded souls would like to but feel incapable of doing so. In other words, Megan fell for men who would have loved to be able to give her what she wanted but felt too broken to deliver the emotional goods. And unlike Daphne and the other RRs from Chapter 3, Megan wasn't trying to prove her worth through her relationships—she was focused on trying to fix her partner, in the hopes that if she put in enough work, she'd have her perfect match, and that their resulting love would be all the more transcendent because of what she'd helped him overcome.

Megan's lovers were not bad men, and you couldn't fairly dismiss them as losers. The truth was more complicated: They were good people who were prevented by a range of obstacles from growing into strong, reliable, and emotionally available partners. Though they were aware of their limitations and wanted to be able to pull their lives together and become emotionally strong, they lacked either the capacity or the motivation to do so. Meanwhile, Megan repeatedly waited in vain, fixated on what her boyfriends could become, never acknowledging that her boyfriends may not ultimately change that much. It was obvious to me—and her friends, too, I'm sure—that time and again she invested all of her energy in the fantasy of who her boyfriend could become in the future as opposed to banking on who he was in the here-and-now.

After Megan had been in a relationship for two or three months, she unfailingly became unhappy. Yet she had grown accustomed to investing in relationships in which she got little in return, and she had virtually stopped believing that love could look any different. Megan loved with all her heart and might, and gave some men a second and third chance when they didn't deserve it. Plain and simple: Wounded souls were her Achilles' heel.

The problem for Megan was that she tried to change her partner— the trademark attempt of people who try to rescue wounded souls. She had hoped that loving Jay well enough could save him and resurrect him so that he could finally be the kind of partner she'd always wanted. Yet the fantasy that her love could transform him never became a reality. And she was so busy trying to heal him that she never zoomed out to give her own behavioral patterns a look, which might have revealed to her that this was a dead-end she'd traversed many times before.

Emotional Fallout

Whether she consciously realized it at the time or not, repeatedly attempting to rescue wounded souls was engulfing Megan in a thick layer of frustration. Even worse, continually reliving this pattern had the additional effect of battering her self-esteem. After not feeling emotionally fulfilled by a partner for such a long time, she began to question whether there was something wrong with her and whether she even deserved to get what she wanted and needed from a man. Her compulsive relationship choices were holding her back, and eating away at months and years during which she could have been establishing a lasting relationship. Sadly, all this time, she could have been building a life with someone and working toward something as opposed to working against herself and her dreams.

Megan was by no means alone in her compulsive repetition. Other RRs who get caught in this pattern similarly come to see their lovers as sympathetic characters, never realizing that the attachment they feel for their partners is often just pity masquerading as something deeper. They don't realize they're supposed to be girlfriends—not therapists or life coaches!

RRs who repeat this pattern fall for individuals who say things like "I don't know why you would want to be with me," or "I'm too messed up for you." People like Megan don't hear a warning in these words—they hear a challenge to dive deep into a relationship, to heal, and to make it work at all costs. In the meantime, RRs focus almost exclusively on what needs to change in their partners, forgetting about focusing on their own needs and what needs to *change in them*. After all, something needs to change in the repeater if the goal is to stop repeating!

One of the most common types of passive wounded souls that RRs try to rescue is addicts. RRs may fall for individuals addicted to alcohol, illicit drugs, prescription drugs, gambling, sex, or food. RRs who love addicts try with all their might to believe that their lovers would be fine if only they could break free from their addictions. Ignoring all the evidence to the contrary is emotionally draining, but these RRs persevere, feeding on a steady diet of denial and creative rationalizations.

Rescuing Aggressive Wounded Souls

Draped in a wispy skirt and surrounded by the waist-length red hair that flowed behind her, Maryann drifted into my office the way I imagined she drifted through life: breezily, with a laid-back air. At forty, she was in the early stages of a new career as a real estate agent and found herself drawn to the flexibility and get-up-and-go nature of her job.

Maryann had been divorced three years earlier. She had met her ex-husband, Jim, when he grabbed her hand and pulled her onto the dance floor at a friend's wedding. He was a tall, broad-shouldered man with a loud laugh and a sure-footed confidence that allowed him to put strangers at ease with his good-natured ribbing. Less than a year later, they held their own wedding reception on that very same dance floor where they'd met.

About a year and a half into their marriage, Maryann noticed that the strength and confidence that had so immediately charmed her took on a different color, and that her husband was actually a very controlling man. Though he still wielded a disarming charm and sweetness when he wanted to, he frequently sent the house's mood plunging into a deep freeze at the most unpredictable provocations. Maryann did what she could to prevent these mood swings, by cutting work appointments short so she could be on time when they met for movies after work, or writing reminders to herself to call him every evening when she was out of town. Yet despite her efforts to cater to his every mood and insecurity, it was never enough. She recalled an episode after she brought home Chinese food on a night he'd planned to grill steaks, and he'd grown beet-faced and lectured her that she "better learn how to listen!" Tired and frustrated, Maryann began to realize that she'd never be able to compile an exhaustive list of all the things that could set Jim off.

Maryann was an easygoing woman, someone who'd always known how to be flexible and to adapt to her circumstances. Initially, she figured that her temperament and what she called her husband's "Type A—with a bold and capital 'A'" personality were complementary—the yin and the yang that could balance each other out. She also knew that, despite his volatile and controlling nature and sometimes aggressive exterior, he was a good man. Maryann spent a lot of time talking to him and listening to him when he got out of control—she was an ace comforter. She believed that there was some sort of unacknowledged pain inside of him that made him lash out, so she was patient in trying to give him enough love to smooth out his rough edges. But after ten patient years of trying to make things better, Maryann left Jim. Her departure marked the culmination of lasting bouts of frustration and anger, work projects suffering, and the sudden wake-up call she received when she responded to an online survey about hobbies and could think of nothing else but "Keeping my husband happy." As she filled out the survey, she initially intended her response as a joke. Yet as she sat there, staring at the screen, she realized that there was nothing funny about the way her husband's mood swings had taken over her life and the fact that her relationship had swallowed her whole.

Maryann spent a year on her own, and then began to date again. She told me that dating triggered insecurities she remembered having as a young girl. I could see that she struggled with low self-esteem that stemmed, in part, from her experience of having a limp that resulted from a childhood injury. Other children had made terrible fun of her, and she never could shake the feeling that she was a perpetual misfit. She said that although she had had the limp corrected with surgery years ago, her social discomfort and her feeling that strangers were snickering behind her back never fully disappeared.

Dating after being married for ten years brought with it the predictable slew of discomforts, but what Maryann found most frightening was the fact that the men with whom she agreed to go on second and third dates inevitably began to remind her of her ex-husband. One of her relationships since the divorce lasted about nine months, and it had ended messily with her refusal to stop catering to her boyfriend's every emotional whim. When she got angry one day and decided she'd had enough, Maryann told him she couldn't take any more of his finding fault with her and everything around them. Her boyfriend had looked at Maryann as though she'd sprouted two heads, taken aback by the outburst after months of nothing but endless hours of patient listening and compromising from her.

Maryann forged relationships with men who were kind at heart but difficult to get along with on a consistent basis. In the beginning, she was drawn to the strength and take-charge confidence she saw in these men. In the end, however, she realized that they were emotionally volatile, reactive, controlling, and jealous.

Had Maryann simply had a relationship with only one man who was controlling and volatile, she could have dismissed her experience as an isolated incident. That she continued to find herself dating similar men after her divorce made her realize that a recurring pattern guided her attraction to men. The pattern—rescuing aggressive wounded souls—is one common to many RRs.

Rescue Does Not Equal Love

Like RRs who settle into relationships with passive wounded souls, RRs who pair up with aggressive wounded souls are trying, through their every action, to change their partners. Unfortunately, however, the RRs who engage in this pattern are usually unaware of this underlying motivation. As a result of that unawareness, they repeat futile attempts to rescue their lovers and inevitably experience disappointment as they're confronted by the fading prospect of healthy, mutual love.

RRs who rescue aggressive wounded souls hope that loving their partners well enough can heal and change them. Maryann's and Megan's boyfriends are different in many ways, but their differences stem from the same seed. While Megan's boyfriend was lost and helpless and Maryann's partners were controlling and volatile, both women's partners were emotionally broken. Though the brokenness manifested differently, both women's lovers were unable to manage their own feelings and function as full-blooded, emotionally strong men. In short, they were unable to function as a healthy, productive 50 percent of a partnership.

Those who repeat this pattern don't fall for these men because they think the men are downright awful. In fact, when their partners are good, they're really good. When they're bad, however, they don't think twice about crossing the RRs' boundaries and indulging any thought or feeling that flies through their heads, regardless of how it might impact their partners. The point is that the RRs seek out and stay in these relationships because they unconsciously are drawn to the rescue— that is what they've come to recognize as love.

THE RESCUER:

- Regularly attaches herself to partners who are emotionally unstable in some way.
- Focuses on and worries more about her partner more than he does about himself.
- Repeatedly finds herself with partners who at first seem to be sweet and have great potential (while also being slightly helpless or misguided), but before long reveal themselves to be emotionally volatile or unstable, aggressive and controlling, unhappy, or unable to cope with some aspect of their lives.
- Often believes that love trumps everything and that ending a relationship would mean giving up on or abandoning the man she loves.
- Desperately tries to help her partner but, at root, is trying to change her partner.
- Tends to have partners with histories of anxiety, depression, or substance abuse.
- Often comes from a family in which she felt the need to take care of a parent or sibling, or in which there was a high level of turmoil and drama.

When I refer to Maryann's ex-husband and boyfriends as aggressive wounded souls, you may think to yourself that they're not aggressive because they never physically hit Maryann. Let me be clear that RRs who repeat this pattern—rescuing aggressive wounded souls—are not necessarily in physically abusive relationships. However, a person isn't required to hit someone to qualify as aggressive. More subtle types of aggression can entail crossing personal boundaries and engaging in volatile or erratic behavior.

One of the saddest consequences for RRs who repeat this pattern is that they start to feel crazy or to doubt themselves in their relationships. The RRs desperately try to figure out their partners in order to determine which stimuli lead to which emotional outcomes, but never quite succeed because their partners' behavior is so confusing and erratic. The RRs start thinking the problem might lie in them. Further, their partners often plant this seed in the RRs by blaming the RRs for their behaviors (saying things like "You bring it out in me," or "You do this to me"). As a result, RRs who repeat this pattern often doubt their own sanity because their partners are constantly changing the rules. They never have real peace in their relationships because they face a constant onslaught of mixed messages and erratic moods.

Here's the good news for the repeaters: RRs who repeat this pattern are often gifted individuals, though they likely don't know it. They tend to be very strong, resilient individuals who are highly intuitive, sensitive, and giving. They understand that their partners are complicated people whose behavior can be difficult to predict.

THE TAKEAWAY

Although Megan and Maryann appear to have very different partners at first glance, a closer look reveals that the men they sought were similarly emotionally broken and dysfunctional. Their partners were wounded souls who needed a great deal of emotional repair before they could engage in a lasting, healthy relationship. Megan, for example, was drawn to men who appeared sweet but were helpless. Without fail, she fell for men who were chock full of potential but who could never ultimately rise to the occasion. Megan is like other RRs who rescue what I call passive wounded souls. On the other hand, Maryann was drawn to men who appeared to be in control, and who had a take-charge quality, though she later found them to be controlling, erratic, and emotionally volatile. Maryann is like other RRs who rescue aggressive wounded souls. There is an in-your-face quality to the partners they choose, and the RRs frequently feel confused and frustrated in their relationships. RRs who have relationships with aggressive wounded souls start to feel crazy and often doubt their sanity in the face of such erratic behavior and mixed messages.

SELF-EVALUATION
Do You Have a Fix-It Mindset?

1. Have you ever tried to rescue a wounded soul? If so, which type? If not, why do you believe this is one pattern you wouldn't fall into?

2. Can you recall a time when you got to know someone and could see that he or she was emotionally broken? How did that affect your developing friendship or relationship? How should it affect your developing relationship?

3. What might the appeal be of forging a relationship with a wounded soul? Why would a person fall for someone who is broken?

4. What are the essential differences between a wounded soul and the average man with typical imperfections?

CHAPTER 5

Pattern #4

Sacrificing Yourself

ALICIA WAS A PRETTY, thirty-seven-year-old woman who, when she first came to see me, cited no central problem in her life, just a "general need for a tune-up." By the second session, it was clear that the part of her life that could most benefit from a mechanic was her long-term relationship with her boyfriend, Mark.

Alicia had been with Mark for about two years, but several months into the relationship, she had already started to feel that something was wrong. The first warning sign she noticed was in the bedroom: He suggested they try a sexual position that she preferred to steer clear of, and though she made her strong reservations known, he kept pushing and trying to get his way. She held out until she thought he'd given up. When the same scenario repeated itself a couple of weeks later, she again said "no," and he stormed out of the room. Alicia was embarrassed to admit that after that, she occasionally gave into him sexually because she wanted to avoid the pouting, the cold shoulders, and the snappishness that always followed her refusals.

"What was I supposed to do?" she asked me. "I wanted to keep the peace."

It was difficult for me to watch her trying to turn something that had "toxic" written all over it into a successful relationship. I explained to her that it seemed she was worrying more about her partner's feelings than either she or her partner were worrying about her own. "You can't expect to have a good relationship when you are willing to sacrifice yourself to make it work," I told her.

Contributing to Alicia's difficulty in identifying Mark's behavior as abusive was the fact that it didn't fit snugly into any single category of abuse that she'd heard of. The truth is that it was a mix: It was both sexual and emotional abuse. Often, the maltreatment that Alicia and many other women have encountered in their relationships rarely fits neatly under the heading of a certain type. Instead, the abuse is more likely a mix of behaviors, and while the women may not know exactly what to call it, they do know that what they're experiencing is confusing, disrespectful, and often frightening.

Abuse by Any Other Name . . .

Penelope, a mild-mannered woman who spoke with a slight Southern accent, had a job she liked in the administrative office of a major cruise line company. After our initial small talk, I asked her why she'd decided to come see me, and she admitted that it hadn't been her idea. One of her friends told her that whether Penelope was willing to admit it or not, her current relationship, with a man named Lawrence, was an abusive one. What's more, her friend pointed out that this wasn't the first time Penelope had been in a dangerously dysfunctional relationship. Penelope's friend offered to pay for the first few counseling sessions if Penelope would just simply give it a try, and Penelope couldn't think of an excuse fast enough to get out of it.

Every time the word "abuse" or "abusive" ran across her lips, she lowered her voice a little.

"Some of my friends use the word 'abuse' so loosely. I hear that word and I think of broken bones, black eyes, sweaters in the summer to hide bruises. That stuff isn't a part of my relationships."

I told her that partners can be abusive in ways that don't involve broken bones, and that it's true that other types of abuse are subtler and can be difficult to label. But that doesn't make those types any less real. Abuse is still serious when it takes the form of verbal attacks or emotional manipulation.

"What do you think makes your friend label your relationship as abusive?" I asked.

Penelope avoided my question at first.

"I've heard about the cycle of abuse," she said, "where people who are abused as children look for abusive relationships as adults. That just doesn't apply to me. I can honestly say I wouldn't change a thing about my childhood." We were both silent for a moment. "Lawrence isn't dangerous or anything, that's why it's so hard for me to think of him as an abuser. He did slap me once, a long time ago, but other than that one time he's never tried to hurt me." She swallowed, still not meeting my eyes. "But I guess he does get mad at me a lot."

Over our next several sessions (she ended up coming to many more than the few her friend offered to pay for), Penelope told me about the different ways Lawrence tended to get mad at her. As she walked me through the examples, I helped her understand why his actions qualified as abuse. There were the verbal attacks (he often called her a "dirty whore" or similar names when she was getting ready to go out with friends), the emotional manipulation (he withheld sex for several nights after she had lunch with a male friend he didn't trust, and wouldn't speak to her for two days when she refused to call in sick to work to take a daytrip with him), and the so-called joking that tended to go too far (he'd recently pinned her down on the bed when she was trying to leave to meet her mom for dinner because he wanted her to stay there with him). Recalling the instance on the bed, Penelope appeared embarrassed to recount the details: As he held her down, she tried to laugh it off at first but found tears welling up moments later. In the end, it seemed, fear always worked its way into their most intense moments.

As we discussed the various behaviors that scared her, Penelope told me that she was struck by how easy it was for me to label which kind of abuse each of these behaviors constituted. Over the course of several months, Lawrence's conduct started to look less like the harmless whims of a temperamental man and more like one big red warning flag.

Penelope eventually admitted that part of the reason Lawrence's abuse had seemed so innocent to her was that all of her serious boyfriends had treated her similarly. In other words, this was her "normal." Tracing back to events that occurred years before this last relationship, she revealed some important details. In fact, the man she called her first real love, a long-term boyfriend she'd had throughout high school, had pushed her down some basement stairs at a party her senior year, causing her to sprain her ankle. She'd broken up with him on the spot, and vowed never to be with a man who abused her like that again. And she hadn't—but she'd unwittingly found the loophole in her inner vow, and found plenty of men who abused her in other ways.

Learned Helplessness

Of course Penelope didn't consciously want to be with men who treated her badly. She meant it when she told herself and her friends that next time she'd find someone different. But before she could do that, she had some mental changes to make.

Somewhere along the way, Penelope had internalized the notion that her partners were treating her the way she deserved to be treated. Over time, the years spent with a stream of abusive partners confirmed and strengthened this belief, until it came to feel normal on some level to be mistreated. How, you might ask yourself, could something so awful start to seem normal? The answer is that what is normal to you is relative. If your relationships have shown you that you will be treated a certain way—bad as it may be—this type of treatment is the only kind you really know. Given that human nature causes us to gravitate toward what is familiar, these RRs may actually avoid situations in which they are treated well because the unfamiliarity could lead to discomfort.

Looking back, Penelope couldn't figure out why she'd stayed with her boyfriends after the first few abusive episodes. I responded by telling her about a landmark study that introduced a condition called "learned helplessness."

I know that telling you about a psychological study of dogs may seem a little strange, but you will soon see how it relates. In the 1960s, researchers J. Bruce Overmier and Martin E. P. Seligman set out to learn what dogs would do in painful situations when they had no control over their circumstances. All the dogs in the study received shocks (for obvious reasons, this is a study that would never be replicated today!). For one group of dogs, pressing a lever prevented the shocks. For other dogs, pressing the lever did nothing. In the end, dogs that could not control whether they got shocked stopped trying to use the lever at all and simply laid down. They accepted the shock because they learned there was nothing they could do to avoid the pain. The experimenters named this reaction "learned helplessness."

RRs who sacrifice themselves in their relationships, I believe, similarly display learned helplessness. After they continue to forge relationships that ultimately become abusive, they feel trapped and afraid, believing that they cannot change the abusive outcomes. Similar to the dogs' reactions, they believe they must lie down and take it. The constant abuse convinces them there is nothing they can do to avoid it. Ultimately, they lose hope that a good relationship exists or that they will ever find one that lasts, and the healthy couples that surround them start to look like shams or actors pretending to be in love. The abuse wears down the sacrificers down to the point that they stop believing pure, kind love between a man and a woman exists. That love—whether between a seemingly perfect couple in real life or a pretend couple on a silly soap opera—is a cruel joke in the beaten-down, exhausted minds of the sacrificers.

THE SACRIFICER:

- Repeatedly has partners who verbally, emotionally, sexually, or physically abuse her.
- Has noticed that her partner's moods tend to leap, without warning, from one end of the spectrum to the other.
- Often fears that one wrong move could trigger her partner to get angry and begin an abusive cycle.
- Sees herself as trapped and betrayed in her relationships, as she feels too guilty to leave and too afraid of what her partner might do if she tried to do so.
- Tries to excuse her partner's abusive behavior by saying things like, "It only happened once," or "He only does it when he gets mad."
- Eventually begins to wonder if she's going insane, because her partner does such an able job of putting the blame on her.
- Loses her grasp on what normal behavior in a relationship looks like and fears that the abuse has damaged her to the point that future healthy lovers wouldn't want to be with her.

THE TAKEAWAY

Repeating the pattern of sacrificing yourself in a relationship has devastating effects. It can lead to confusion, depression, and anxiety, and can cause or reinforce a cursed or damaged identity. RRs who sacrifice themselves forge relationships with men who verbally, emotionally, or physically abuse them. Why these individuals get into abusive relationships in the first place is complicated. The reality is that someone does not get into such a relationship for one reason only; there are several factors that are likely to be at work. RRs can get into these relationships because of a combination of low self-esteem, severe avoidance of conflict, a past traumatic history, or overdependence on their romantic partners. Why RRs stay in abusive relationships relates, in part, to a reaction called "learned helplessness." The pattern of sacrificing oneself in an abusive relationship is so destructive that the only way for the RR to stop the abusive cycle is to leave the relationship for good and change the way she thinks about—and approaches—relationships. Once we get to the exercises in the next two parts of the book, you will find that there are a host of new behaviors, and a good deal of self-exploration, that you can engage in that will help you stop repeating this pattern forever.

SELF-EVALUATION
Recognizing Abuse

1. Has anyone ever mistreated you in any of the ways discussed in this chapter? If not, how have you avoided relationships with such partners?

2. What would you do if someone new were to abuse you in some way—emotionally, verbally, or physically?

3. What do you think is the hardest type of abuse to spot and label in other people's relationships? What would be the hardest type to label if it were your own relationship?

CHAPTER 6

The Big Four

The Underlying Causes of RRS

NOW THAT YOU HAVE a solid grasp on the patterns RRs repeat, as well as the types of lovers they're compulsively drawn to, we're ready to take a look at the sources feeding the compulsion. In other words, we'll delve into how it applies in your case: Why and how did you get stuck repeating in the first place? This chapter will shed light—hopefully of the high-intensity variety—on the possible answer to that question so that you can begin to understand yourself better and gain total control over your romantic relationships.

At its root, repeating the same bad relationship patterns is self-sabotaging behavior. It's difficult for someone who is not an RR to understand why anyone would continue to engage in behavior that makes them feel worse in the end, and that's a valid quandary; the answer probably isn't even clear to you as an RR yourself. Let's take a walk through the rocky terrain of these complex behaviors. Once we've begun the process of charting the territory, it won't look nearly as ominous.

Just as there are different versions of dysfunctional relationship patterns that you repeat, there are different reasons why you keep repeating the behavior. No one reason corresponds with any one pattern—you'll do some mixing and matching as you figure out which pattern and reason best fit you. You'll quickly find that it's not always a simple equation. In fact, you might be compelled to repeat your relationship behavior due to a cocktail of reasons listed in the following sections, with strong doses of some drivers mixing with weaker doses of others. But when it comes right down to it, every RR repeats due to one or more of these four underlying causes. As you read about each, tune your intuition to my explanations and pay attention to which explanations speak to you and your circumstances.

Reason #1: Fear

Fear is the pushy puppeteer controlling us in so many aspects of our lives. Hands down, it is one of the most persistent barriers to finding lasting love. Read about the different manifestations of fear that follow and ask yourself whether this manipulative emotion might be fueling your own self-sabotaging behavior.

Fear of Having a Good Relationship

The title of this section may not make sense to you—but hold on. Most people expect that a good relationship makes you feel better and decreases your anxiety, but if you're an RR, that's not necessarily the case. In fact, given your penchant for repeating your behavior and consorting with the wrong partners, your anxiety level can actually spike in a good relationship!

It should be said that many people—RRs or not—deal with this contradiction on some level. Psychologists explain that positive emotions, like openness and joy, actually make us feel more vulnerable than negative emotions, even though they're far healthier for us to sustain over time. Fear and sadness have protective qualities, meaning that they cause you to withdraw and put up walls against the world in order to make yourself feel safe and secure. On the other hand, positive emotions potentially expose you to rejection and pain, which can be a terrifying prospect if you've experienced heartbreak. The prospect is even more terrifying if you've grown accustomed to heartbreak and know little else when it comes to love.

As an RR, you simply don't know how a good relationship works after years of surviving dysfunctional ones. You are likely not able to recognize a healthy bond. How could you, if you've never seen one up close? Given its unfamiliarity, you may feel terrified and anxious in a good relationship. In this way, fear diligently does its job, helping you avoid men who are good partners for you and keeping you running toward those who aren't. At least with a bad relationship, you know what to predict, right?

Fear of Intimacy

Whether you're aware of it or not, as an RR, you actively avoid intimacy as you cycle through one bad relationship after another. Through this process, you can develop a tremendous fear of intimacy. The prospect of a *real* relationship—and real intimacy—can kick-start all sorts of anxious turmoil for RRs.

When I first introduce the concept of intimacy to my patients, they often appear confused and think that intimacy only relates to sexual feelings and acts. The truth is that there is the potential for intimacy in every relationship—between parents and children, between siblings, and between friends and lovers, among others.

WHAT IS INTIMACY?

Intimacy refers to a mutual wish to know one another and to care for one another, as well as the ability to share vulnerability and trust each other. RRs may have had experiences earlier in life that taught them it's not safe to trust, love, or be vulnerable. Many RRs have learned to be fairly self-sufficient, despite giving off the impression that they are wrapped up in their relationships and overly dependent on others to be happy. But it's easy to be misled by what you see on the surface: the self-sufficiency is a by-product of the belief that no one else will care for them and meet their needs. Accordingly, they learn to do so themselves. In this way, they protect their feelings like castles on the hill, surrounded by a moat and a creaky drawbridge.

Many RRs have a fear of intimacy because they had no instruction manual for intimacy earlier in life. If you were born and raised with most all of your emotional needs met and cared for, intimacy and trust in relationships is probably a no-brainer. However, not everyone had it so easy. When I see RRs in my office, I am usually confident that they don't trust for good reason—something hurtful probably struck them down a long time ago.

Naturally, these RRs want to avoid intimacy because it is foreign territory for them. Many RRs are simply terrified they won't survive.

Reason #2: Denial

In our everyday lives, we use some words or concepts so liberally that we lose sight of their true meanings. How would you define "denial"? You may find that my definition is subtly, but crucially, different from yours.

If you are in denial of something, you are not fully aware of it. This lack of awareness is not angry defensiveness or a refusal to admit something that you know is true. Slow down for a moment to think about the important difference between awareness and denial.

Denial is a defense mechanism your mind produces to defend against a powerful and unpleasant emotional force. When something is too upsetting, your mind will push it out of your consciousness so that you do not become overwhelmed or destroyed by the emotions. Your mind produces the defense mechanism of denial to shut out the feelings—to protect you. Imagine the moat surrounding the castle that I talked about earlier. In this respect, denial is the moat and the castle is you. When you understand the function of this defense mechanism, you can better understand how your mind works in covert ways to protect you.

Denial of Emotional Needs

After hearing the stories of the RRs in the past chapters, and thinking about your own situation, you know that repeating relationships makes an RR feel bad—anxious, angry, and depressed. Why would you keep repeating hurtful relationship patterns if hurt is always the end result? Are you a masochist? Do you like feeling the pain? The easy answer is no, but the more complicated answer revolves around what most RRs have in common: You are out of touch with your emotional needs.

When we talk about needs, we usually talk about physical needs like water, food, and shelter. However, I firmly believe that the emotional needs we have as humans are almost equally important. Henry Murray, a famous psychologist known for his list of basic human needs, focused on the need for affiliation. This need, described in his 1938 book *Explorations in Personality,* refers to the need to be close to and have trust in others.

This need for affiliation is critical to a healthy, balanced mind and outlook on the world. We need love, and we need to give love. However, for some people, it's easier and less risky to love a pet, for instance, than it is to love a person. For these individuals, it is easier to acknowledge their need for their pet than it is to acknowledge the messier, more pressing emotional needs they have—those involving other humans.

While most would agree that we need to feel close with other people, some may not regularly reflect on what their primary emotional needs are in relationships, and whether those needs are being met. Simply maintaining a relationship, even a long-term one, does not automatically mean that this need for intimacy and real companionship is satisfied!

HOW DOES THIS APPLY UNIQUELY TO RRS?

If you're an RR, your emotional needs may have gone unmet for so long that you've forgotten you even have them. Even worse, you may never have had these needs met from the very beginning. Given a missing template, you can't comprehend the concept of meeting true, core, primary needs on any emotional level. You may be apt to intellectualize your way out of your feelings, or rationalize that you simply don't have the needs so many others have. In such instances, the red blinking arrow is clearly pointing directly at denial. Consider what a true tragedy this is: You are often in denial of the greatest emotional needs humans have.

Think about it. If I were to ask you what you're looking for in a partner and in a relationship, my guess is that you'd deliver a neat and simplistic response. Sometimes what you're looking for is a fantasy. Or you may be working with a checklist of items (straight teeth, a PhD, no obnoxious family members) that are unfortunately not at all based on meaningful factors.

Most RRs have lacked intimacy for so long that they have no idea what it would feel like to get what they need emotionally. It's not that they don't want to find partners who will treat them well, but they long ago called off the loving-partner hunt, believing that those types of lovers must be an extinct species. RRs have gotten to the point at which:

- Imagining being treated well is a foreign concept.
- Imagining being happy and fulfilled in a relationship is inconceivable.
- Imagining having peace of mind in a relationship is not even considered.

In Chapter 2, I pointed out the characteristics that Valerie omitted in describing her ideal partner: kind, stable, respectful. Shouldn't these be at the top of anyone's list? Of course. It's not that the RR has shallow or poor values, but rather, she is simply out of touch with her own emotional needs.

Denial of Old Feelings

RRs often keep repeating, in part, because they are in denial of their feelings. Not only is it possible for them to stay in the same kinds of relationships because of denial of their own needs, but it's also possible that they're in denial of painful old feelings such as anger or sadness.

Anger

Some RRs may repeat because they are in denial of unresolved anger, which could have become turned inward on themselves. If some experience or person deeply hurt you in the past, you may have been awash in anger for a long time as a result of having been treated unfairly or wrongly. And you may not realize it, but the truth is that *if not expressed appropriately, deep anger doesn't go away.*

I tell my patients "It always finds a place to go," and that "It will inevitably come out in some other way." Anger only goes away once there has been some resolution. Some RRs are not able to express their anger toward the person in the situation in which they were wronged or in the situation that provoked the anger. Because anger is like a pressure buildup, and the pressure's force must go somewhere, the anger valve can break and, for all its messiness, be contained internally.

When anger gets misdirected, it shifts and moves around in an unconscious process. Obviously you would not intend for this to happen if you could control it. But anger makes its presence known: Sometimes, the anger doesn't peter out, and instead keeps fueling the repetition of unhappy relationships later in life. You might engage in self-destructive behavior to punish yourself, the only way you know how to make sense of the complex maze of anger and frustration you have carried with you all these years after having been wronged in the past.

Sadness

Some RRs repeat because they are in denial of a deep, old sadness. You may have harbored this sadness for many years after a significant wounding experience. You're in denial of the sadness because your mind has pushed it out of your consciousness. This process could have occurred for two reasons.

First, the wounding experience may have occurred when you were so young that you cannot recall the experience. Second, the wounding experience could be too painful to be allowed through the door of awareness and acknowledgment. Accordingly, your mind may have pushed the experience from conscious awareness out of a fear that acknowledging it could devastate you. Later in life, you may find yourself repeating unhappy relationships because the sadness induced by the current relationship feels familiar and aligns with the deep sadness you have unknowingly carried for many years. The current sadness is in sync with the old sadness.

The RR who repeats for this reason does so because she is unaware of the depth of sadness that lies beneath the surface. If you carry old sadness with you today, your unhappy relationships give rise to hurt feelings and sadness that feel familiar to all the old hurt and pain that has been simmering for so long. Though the sadness is not exactly comfortable, it feels familiar—and people always gravitate toward what is familiar because it feels like home. Sadly, home for some RRs is a place that feels sad and lost, uncared for and lonely.

Denial of Your Own Accountability

While some RRs repeat because they are in denial of the old anger or sadness they carry, other RRs repeat for a different but related reason. In a word, it boils down to accountability. It's entirely possible that you repeat bad relationship patterns because of a basic lack of accountability for your fair share in a relationship. More specifically, you do not hold yourself accountable for why things went wrong in your relationship and instead opt to blame your partner. If you fall into this category, you're failing to acknowledge that you're a participant in the relationship dynamic and that you signed up for—at least, to some degree—the dysfunctional dynamics of the relationship. In other words, you don't realize you are responsible for 50 percent of the relationship, and you refuse to ask yourself what behavior you could have changed to yield a more positive relationship outcome. Remember: *ignorance is not bliss.* When it comes to relationships, ignorance ultimately equals unhappiness.

I realize that denial of your own accountability is no easy pill to swallow, but seriously consider whether this has been a barrier in your relationships and is the reason you keep repeating. If it is not, keep reading to see which reason better applies to you. If it is, know that the rest of this book offers a prescription to help relieve you from your old ways and to set you on a course of positive change.

Reason #3: Impulsive Coping Style

Some RRs keep repeating their relationships because, quite simply, they are impulsive people. While some personalities may be timid or rigid, cautious or anxious, other personalities bring traces—or heaps—of impulsivity to the table. Impulsive personalities are prone to behavior without thinking in advance of how the consequences will affect them. As an impulsive RR, you may engage in this kind of behavior because you are uncomfortable sitting long with certain feelings like boredom, sadness, or anger. So, without often pausing to reflect on or distance yourself from a situation, you tend to jump to action. It is this quickness that can lead to destructive outcomes. If this sounds like you, you are, in a word, a doer. You don't like to sit tight; you'd rather do something. You'd rather act.

Some RRs repeat relationships because they impulsively start a relationship without appropriately vetting their partners first—they jump in too fast. Impulsive RRs find themselves stuck in unhappy relationships and don't understand that they got there because they jumped in without sufficient care and attention to their partners' emotional traits.

In addition, impulsive RRs often have short relationships rather than long-term relationships because they feed on action. Would you rather switch relationships every so often because you get bored or frustrated if you're in the same one for too long? Again, because impulsive RRs prefer behavior to feelings, they'd always rather *do* something—and ending, starting, or switching relationships is easier than sitting with the feelings that get stirred up in an intimate relationship that lasts. Sooner or later, impulsive RRs need to break free. Impulses are like a sugar rush to these RRs—impulses propel them to action, and acting is what makes them feel alive.

Drawn to Drama

Some RRs who are impulsive also find themselves in relationships marked by emotional highs and lows. These RRs can engage in extreme behaviors, which can run the gamut from emotional outbursts (screaming, sudden exits from social situations) to excessive drug or alcohol abuse, from infidelity to physical violence (toward objects, themselves, or others).

If you are an RR who has a history of dramatic relationships, perhaps you originally came from a home where there was a high degree of emotion or conflict. Other RRs may have a biological predisposition to a mood imbalance, and they act out in dramatic ways because they are unable to regulate their moods. For these RRs, dramatic behavior can almost act as a relief valve when the internal pressure gets to be too much.

After years of having gone through dramatic relationships, rationalization often sets in. With time as a buffer, you can see your extreme behavior, along with the extreme and excessive reunions (great make-up sex, almost poetic verbal expressions of love) as *real* love. In other words, big drama equals big love.

This behavior, however, does not mean that you love drama. To suggest that women who are prone to dramatic relationships love drama is patronizing and unfair. The real reason why you may repeat is that you have come to see the highs and lows as part of life, as an expression of the uniqueness of your relationship. You're afraid that a good relationship equals stability, that stability equals boredom, and that boredom equals emotional death. You convince yourself that you don't want someone who is "too nice" and that you can only be sexually attracted to people who are bad for you emotionally. Deep down, however, no one truly wants chaos. The bottom line is that RRs don't love drama at all—they tolerate it. Many RRs tolerate drama because they are afraid they couldn't *tolerate* stability. In this way, denial of an impulsive coping style and need for drama seriously interferes with their happiness and relationships.

Addictive Tendency

Repeating some behaviors is harmless, while repeating others is harmful. What makes some behaviors take on an addictive quality? When the behaviors take on a self-destructive quality, when you repeatedly settle into the wrong relationship, there is a reality you must face: *There can be an addictive quality to the way you repeat relationships.*

One criterion that characterizes addiction is the wish to be able to stop a behavior, despite the fact that the urge to engage in it is more powerful and usually wins out. In terms of repeating unhealthy relationship patterns, the addictive quality is introduced when you continue to engage in behavior that you know is not good for your, or that you know will lead to an unhappy result. For the vast majority of RRs, repeating relationships may simply reflect an addictive tendency that leads them to engage in behaviors that aren't good for them. But for others, repeating relationships may spur mounds of drama that allows the RR to mask a more serious addiction issue.

Quick disclaimer: I am not suggesting that you would be clinically diagnosed as an addict. A true addict has a wide range of serious symptoms, some of which are medical (e.g. increased tolerance and withdrawal). A subgroup of RRs, however, may have become so busy repeating their relationships because they are actually avoiding another, more typical addiction.

In the background of the romantic brouhaha, do you use alcohol and/or drugs to self-medicate? Has drinking and drug use become a way of coping with life in general? For some RRs in denial of their impulsive coping style, impulsivity gets manifested in both their relationship repeating and in another type of dependency—chemical or otherwise.

If you repeat the same bad relationship patterns, look carefully at your drug and alcohol use and check your eating, shopping, and gambling tendencies, as well. In the end, be sure to ask yourself whether your repeating relationship behavior might actually be masking a different type of addictive tendency (to gambling, overeating, etc.).

Reason #4: Distorted Beliefs

You're not crazy. But let's consider for a moment that some of your beliefs might be a little . . . off. This acknowledgment shouldn't feel like resignation to a life looking through a distorted lens. Instead, the discovery of some not-quite-right fundamental beliefs should feel liberating. No one ever fixed a problem without first identifying what the problem was. When you repeat the same toxic relationship patterns, you must examine your thought processes and beliefs, because they are the foundation for all behavior—including the behavior you engage in when it comes to your relationships.

Unrealistic Expectations

RRs often believe that a relationship will permanently change the way they feel, for the better. They often believe that they will automatically:

1. Feel happy and fulfilled
2. Have a companion who is always there
3. Have a consistently gratifying sex life
4. Be "swept away" from the mundane realities of everyday life

Many Hollywood films reinforce all of these toxic fantasies. *Pretty Woman,* for example, suggests that a single female prostitute can morph into a fulfilled and adored wife the moment she meets the right man. This fantasy reinforces one particular type of relationship repetition: the RR who is drawn to a certain socioeconomic status of a man. In the film, Richard Gere supposedly typifies everything a girl could possibly want—he's wealthy, handsome, and adoring of his lover. But wait, there's a problem: he can't handle intimacy so he pays hookers to keep him company. Come and get it, ladies! That's attractive, right? And yet how many millions of women swooned over his character, paying more attention to the external package than his internal character traits?

Pretty Woman has become an iconic film, underscoring how the public loves a good fantasy. The need for fantasy is understandable enough, given how complex and difficult reality can be. Yet the fantasy in the film's premise is akin to the kind of expectations some RRs have for their relationships. It is my hope that after reading this book, you—as a recovering RR—can appreciate the film's lightheartedness and simultaneously acknowledge how its plot *defies* reality. It is my hope that you trade the fantasies for healthy expectations so that, when you meet a new man, you forget the glitz or the superficial turn-ons and instead ask yourself these questions:

- Is he ready for a relationship?
- Is he motivated by his work and by the various relationships with friends and family in his life?
- Does he communicate his needs well and show an interest in mine?

Asking these questions is much less exciting than waiting for a gorgeous man to pull up in a fancy car with an armful of flowers, but the right answers to these questions will make you much happier in the end!

Pathological Core Beliefs

If you feel strongly that your expectations for your partners are realistic and healthy, take a moment and reflect on whether your core beliefs are possibly interfering with your ability to find and maintain a long-term, positive relationship.

Judith Beck, a psychologist who has written extensively on the concept of core beliefs, asserts in her book *Cognitive Therapy* that core beliefs are "one's most central ideas about the self." In a nutshell, the idea is that a person's dysfunctional behavior may stem from core beliefs that fit into one of these three categories:

1. Do you believe you are unlovable?
2. Do you believe you are helpless?
3. Do you believe a combination of the two?

It may sound like a cliché to suggest that repeating relationships stems from not feeling good enough. But sometimes truth lies in simplicity.

Some RRs may believe in their heart of hearts that they don't deserve a lasting relationship or are inherently incapable of having one. In the next part of the book, we will break down these beliefs so that you can determine if that is all or part of the reason why you repeat bad relationship patterns.

Cognitive Rigidity

This concept is probably new to you, but it will soon make sense. As RRs restrict themselves to a narrow selection of partners—seeking out only emotionally broken men, wealthy men, the list goes on—their way of looking at their relationships may be restrictive, too. RRs may have difficulty seeing relationships in perspective. They may not look at the big picture, and instead get caught up in the details about a relationship or their partner.

Socially, some people appear more easygoing and flexible, while others appear more constrained and rigid. Just as these personality styles are reflected on the surface in social interactions, there may be an equivalent pattern at work in their minds. The way someone thinks and organizes information may be rigid or concrete, or it may be adaptive and flexible.

Let's consider an autistic person, for example. The autistic individual may engage in a particular behavior for minutes on end because his or her brain gets stuck conducting the same repetitive behavior. In a different but related manner, someone who suffers from Obsessive-Compulsive Disorder (OCD) may engage in a set of behavioral rituals and may get stuck conducting certain rituals—counting, checking, or cleaning. While the OCD sufferer is engaging in this behavior, her mind is stuck on the task and cannot be easily redirected to stop. You must understand that this autistic repetition or compulsive repetition is not willful behavior—it's not simply that the individuals choose to do it. For these individuals, the neurological or chemical makeup in their brains causes them to repeat. And repeat. And repeat.

Repeating dead-end relationships may reflect a predisposition to engage in a similar type of compulsive, non–goal-directed behavior. Please note that I am not suggesting a possible diagnosis of autism or OCD. I am suggesting, however, that there is a spectrum of mental pathology, and that the RR may suffer from some of the characteristics that are seen in full-blown disorders involving cognitive rigidity or repetitive behaviors.

Again, if this describes you, don't despair! Examination of the repeating behavior in your relationships through the larger lens of more serious disorders can help remind you that your behavior may stem partly from the way your brain—or mind—works.

Traumatic Mastery

In the mental health field, we often talk about a theory known as faulty or traumatic mastery. The theory concerns how people react after they have been the victims of a traumatic event. Keep in mind that, by definition, a person experiencing a traumatic event likely has no control over what's happening. Faulty mastery, as discussed in a 1999 study by Raymond Flannery, a clinical psychologist who has researched post-traumatic stress disorder extensively, is a concept that explains how some victims later function as a result of the trauma. Flannery says, in essence, that some victims who have experienced a trauma appear to gain some mastery over the original traumatic event by putting themselves in similar traumatic situations later.

It is critical to understand that trauma is not limited to catastrophic events, such as the attack on the Twin Towers on September 11, 2001. While a national catastrophe certainly qualifies as traumatic, other less obvious events can be traumatic as well.

How you define whether an event is traumatic is based on the perception of the person who experiences it.

For example, an extremely sensitive child who is the target of terrible bullying can experience the bullying as traumatic. While some kids may blow off this experience and move on, other kids—based on their personality and biological predispositions—can suffer a trauma as a result.

Traumatic mastery can also extend to relationships. It may be that you repeat bad relationships because you were neglected, rejected, or abandoned in some way in the past that was traumatic for you. Placing yourself in another bad or unfulfilling relationship later in life may be your unconscious—yet faulty—attempt to re-create the original trauma, so that this time you can come out on the winning side. The goal is to master or overcome the original trauma. When you consider the possible reason that makes you repeat, open yourself up to the idea that your relationship repeating may stem from very old, traumatic wounds.

THE TAKEAWAY

There are four common drivers of relationship repeating: fear, denial, an impulsive coping style, and distorted beliefs. One of these reasons or a combination of them can explain why you repeat. Identifying which applies to you is crucial for the next step—beginning to solve the repetition problem.

SELF-EVALUATION
Identify Your RR Triggers

1. Which reason best fits why you repeat? (Hint: If you think none of them fits you, go back and read about denial!)

2. What in your life could have set the stage for you to repeat for that reason?

3. Do you believe you can truly change the underlying causes of your behavior?

PART II

Winning Formula—
The Prescription for Change

CHAPTER 7

Insight

The First Step

BY NOW, YOU ARE already well on your way to changing how you approach your romantic relationships. You started by picking up this book and kept the ball rolling by reading the first part. Please keep in mind that you can take this journey at your own pace and that this book will serve as your gentle guide, ultimately leading you one huge step closer to a relationship that is fulfilling and lasting.

By adopting the prescription in this book, you will follow a simple model based on how change occurs. My enthusiastic support of this model traces back to my second year in graduate school; specifically, to the first week of fall class and a hot, sweaty day in New York City, where I went to school.

That day, my professor first asked his new, intellectually hungry class, "What does it take for a person to change?" We were stumped. What a question—so simple but so bewilderingly complex!

What followed in that class was a discussion about the key elements of change—elements that went on to form the basis of all the clinical work that I do. I learned that the model for change is, in fact, elegantly simple:

Insight + Behavior Change = Identity Change

Let's break it down: First, you must have the insight to become aware of the specific problem you have, so that you can change your behaviors and create a new identity—that of someone who does not engage in the problem behavior you had in the beginning. The idea is that people engage in problematic behaviors—in this case, repeating toxic relationship patterns—because they come to see themselves as practically programmed to engage in that behavior. In other words, you engage in the destructive behaviors because they're woven into your identity—you see yourself, on some level, as a person who would do that kind of thing.

By following the model and engaging in the exercises in my prescription, you can change your relationship identity. Your new insight and behaviors will conspire to help you see yourself differently, as someone who is capable of a good, lasting relationship and, moreover, as someone who will accept nothing less.

Together, let's delve deeper into the insight component so that you move one step closer to your end goal. Before we get to Part III, which asks you to fill out your own insight inventories, I'm going to give you examples of how other RRs have arrived at their own "Aha!" moment—that instant where it all clicks, the light bulb glows, and you let out a triumphant "That's it!"—which will help set the stage for you to dig through your own relationship history and achieve that moment for yourself.

The Breakthrough

Just as they say "Rome wasn't built in a day," I can tell you that insight can't be bought and shipped overnight. The process of becoming aware of your behaviors, thoughts, and feelings takes time. Think for a moment about how you build a house—you start by laying the concrete foundation and build from there. When it comes to learning how to change for the better, you start by gaining insight, which forms the foundation of all your future behavior. You wouldn't want to start building the first level of a house before the concrete foundation has finished drying, and you'll need to have similar patience as you're laying your new insight foundation.

The insight stage involves what I call "The Breakthrough," which is when you become aware of the pattern you repeat and begin to understand how you got stuck repeating that particular pattern. Let's take a look at how recovered RRs—those who have gone through the very journey you're on now—first developed transformative insight into their repetitive behavior and the partners they chose.

Patricia

You'll remember Patricia, my idealizer friend who worked at the makeup counter at a high-end department store. Successful, slightly older men were her romantic Achilles' heel. When she came into my office for the first several sessions, Patricia appeared guarded and nervous, sinking into the couch with her arms folded in front of her and rarely meeting my eyes. She admitted that she was somewhat uncomfortable with the idea of counseling and only decided to try it after her friends persuaded her to try it.

"I'm not sure why I have to be sitting in this office when my friends are out there enjoying their great relationships—relationships that just look so *easy*," she said, shaking her head.

I asked her to describe the men she had loved in her life, and asked her to help me look for common denominators. It was clear, she responded immediately, that she was drawn to ambitious men, but she felt that this was not the problem.

"No," I agreed, "this isn't the problem. The problem may be that this is your number one priority as opposed to one of many."

Patricia fought me on this at first, insisting that she was also careful to make sure they treated her well and were emotionally stable.

"Is that all it takes—stability and ambition? What about a connection and similar interests?" I asked. Patricia furrowed her brow, and then said of course she felt a connection with these men—at least in the beginning.

"Let's talk more about that connection then," I said. I asked her to describe the ways in which she felt connected to the men she'd loved.

"Well," she said, "we couldn't wait to see each other in the beginning and always spent as much time together as possible." Anyone can relate to where she was coming from—it's an electric time in the beginning of a relationship, when mystery and fantasy surround your new partner.

"What you're describing sounds great and is very normal, but you might be talking more about the giddy rush and the sexual attraction that come with a new relationship," I said. "I'm wondering about the emotional connection that you had with these men. Did they see people and the world in a way that was similar to you? Did you truly 'get' each other, as they say?" Patricia shifted her gaze to a spot on the wall above my head, lost in thought.

It appeared that she had not focused on this priority—the emotional connection—and so we needed to focus on it in our work together. Patricia's breakthrough came when she met my gaze again and asked me to explain more about what I meant by "emotional connection." She didn't know it yet, but she had just made her most significant step toward insight so far, and was finally openly examining and acknowledging her needs and what she wanted out of a relationship. From that point on, she asked a lot more questions in our work together and became more active in figuring out how to change her relationships for the better.

Daphne

As you heard Daphne's story—the emotional chaser who loved old movies and stayed too long with men who clearly weren't ready to commit—you could probably empathize with her frustration. She'd grown tired of waiting on men who hemmed and hawed about settling down while daydreams about married life occupied growing portions of her time.

Daphne and I got down to work quickly. She knew what she wanted—and I knew how to help her. Some RRs have already identified which patterns they repeat; for others, that acknowledgment comes later in the process toward change. Daphne fell somewhere in the middle between those two extremes. It took a little bit of digging at first, but we soon found what we were looking for.

Daphne looked sheepish as she walked me through the different relationships she'd had. Her eyes welled with tears as she asked me, "Do you think it's me? Do you think it's something I do that pushes men away?"

Her question didn't surprise me, because this is often the explanation RRs concoct when they can't understand why the one they love won't give them what they want.

I truthfully answered, "I don't think it has anything to do with you not being interesting or attractive enough." But reassurances alone wouldn't help her change.

"Daphne, tell me something: Were each of these men absolutely available to you and interested in settling down from the beginning, and then they changed later?"

Daphne thought about this for a minute and then said, "No, they seemed to be a little aloof and removed from the start, but I thought they were just playing it cool. That's what people do when a relationship is new." I told Daphne something I heard someone say a long time ago: Visualize a camera and take a mental picture of the person you're dating exactly as he functions today—warts and all—and ask yourself: If he never changed, would you still want to be with him in five years?

Daphne looked surprised at this notion, straightening a little and insisting, "Well, no, but people change." Yes, I said, people can of course change, and often do, but they only change when *they* initiate that change—not when others pressure them to do so. I went on, explaining, "You waited around hoping that you would be enough to make him settle down—that you could be enough to change him."

Daphne had never before realized what she was doing in all of those relationships—waiting and hoping she could be enough to change her partner. "When you say it like that, it seems kind of sad and pathetic," she said, lowering her chin.

"It's only sad," I said, "that you sold yourself short in the process of finding love. You can't emotionally chase someone and expect that they will ever be fully available for you to love." Finally, I said, "Hesitation on your partner's part is a different version of 'no,' but it still means 'no.'"

This moment was the breakthrough for Daphne, as she realized that there was a label for what she had been suffering. She gained insight into her behavior by focusing on her own motivations for once, rather than trying to figure out what her partner was thinking, or trying to make him change. This moment marked the first significant step toward ending the old, self-destructive relationship patterns and catapulting Daphne into the throes of meaningful change.

Megan

When you hear more about Megan's story, you might at first be struck by how similar she is to Daphne, but by the end of her story you will see the critical difference. As I have said before, all RRs share something in common—their relationship repeating—but there are important variances in what motivates them to repeat.

Megan, the art gallery receptionist who grew up in a house with a father who drank too much and a mother she had to comfort, was eager in counseling from the start. She was tired of feeling unhappy in her relationships and desperately wanted answers. "My last relationship nearly broke me," she said. "I gave so much and got so little in return in the end." She spoke about her past relationships and explained that the most upsetting part of her relationships ending was that she couldn't blame her boyfriends. Megan always focused on their potential rather than who they were at the present point in time—a very dangerous approach to relationships.

"So you know the pattern you repeat, right?" I asked.

She nodded confidently. "I know I'm drawn to guys who have problems." This was an important step, because identifying which pattern you repeat is the starting point in learning to stop repeating.

The next step was a little trickier. I asked if she knew why she was attracted to such men, and she was a little less sure. "I guess because I want to fix them," she said.

Megan was partly right—she was drawn to wounded men. She always found herself falling in love with men who carried a lot of emotional baggage and who had not done the work to resolve their emotional problems. However, she was missing the other part—why she needed to fix the men she loved. Megan wasn't sure what motivated her to do this and shook her head, frustrated, as if she were letting herself down.

"Maybe if you could fix him," I started, "then he could finally be the partner you've longed for, and you could finally have a mutual, functional, and adult partner." Megan said that this explanation seemed strange—like she was his therapist or something.

Megan's breakthrough didn't come until after the session ended. When she came in for the next session, she said that a sad song she once shared with a boyfriend had triggered thoughts about what we'd talked about in our previous appointment and brought about the "Aha!" moment when she finally gained insight into why she needed to fix her boyfriends. As she had listened to the sappy song, she realized that in some strange way, she felt most in love with men who had an air of tragedy about them, men who seemed like they needed her care. She discovered that part of her believed that if she could bring out the potential in these wounded souls, she'd have a real testament to their love—one she felt she couldn't ever have if she chose someone who was strong in the beginning. But it struck Megan for the first time that a girlfriend's job isn't to fix; it's to live and coexist happily and functionally. Her experiences with her failed relationships had proved to her that no amount of loving and giving can heal someone who doesn't do the healing work himself.

As I mentioned earlier, you will see similarities and differences in the patterns of the women you read about. Though the partners of both Megan (who rescued) and Daphne (who emotionally chased) looked similar because they were both unavailable, the men were unavailable for different reasons. I mentioned earlier that while the partners of women who emotionally chase men don't want to be available or to settle down, the partners of women who rescue wounded souls want to be able to commit but feel too broken to do so. Now, as you read about Penelope, see if you can detect the similarities and differences between her and the others.

Penelope

You'll remember Penelope, the sacrificer who found herself in an abusive relationship with her partner Lawrence. Lawrence had manipulated Penelope into believing that she provoked him to engage in his abusive behavior, and she sought counseling with me when she became afraid that she'd lose her mind completely if she didn't get some help.

Penelope and I spent time in the first few sessions piecing together parts of her relationships with past boyfriends so that we could have a clear picture of what type of partners she sought and fell for. While she explained that each of her past boyfriends was very different from the others, I suggested we focus on what they all had in common—they mistreated her, whether physically, verbally, or emotionally. While her first serious boyfriend once scared her by shouting and reddening when he was angry and ultimately pushed her down a short flight of stairs, her next boyfriend gave her the silent treatment for days when she didn't feel like having sex with him. The pattern was clearly established and culminated in her last boyfriend, who slapped her hard on one occasion, verbally abused her, and pinned her to the bed a few different times when he had too much to drink.

Penelope was a woman who always tended to avoid conflict. When I pointed out the commonality I saw in her relationship history, however, she asked brusquely, "So what are you trying to say?" She wasn't sure where the session was going and she needed some relief from the uncertainty. "What I'm saying is that all of your partners are abusers in some way, and that it's probably not just due to chance," I explained.

"Are you saying it was my fault?" She became visibly upset—hurt and angry that I would somehow suggest she was guilty. I was quick to reassure her because my intent was not to assign blame or guilt. My goal was to help her understand how and why she repeatedly found herself involved with men who mistreated her. After all, if abuse escalates, it can be life threatening. I wanted to help Penelope end her cycle of repeated relationships before she suffered any more.

"Penelope, I'm saying that you are drawn to men who mistreat you because, on some level, abuse is what you expect from a relationship. It's possible that you believe, in some dark, musty corner of your mind, that you don't deserve anything better," I told her gently.

Abuse is one of the trickiest issues to face, both for the victims and for the therapists who treat them. The truth is that no one ever asks to be hit or abused, but we also must understand what motivates a victim to seek out the partner she is with when there already is an established pattern of abuse in the victim's life and, second, to stay in the relationship after the first couple of abusive episodes. Only when the RR has gained insight into these factors will she stop repeating this destructive—and sometimes life-threatening—pattern.

The Difference Between a Bond and Love

When I suggested to Penelope the possibility of leaving her relationship immediately, I hit a brick wall at a hundred miles per hour. She was nowhere near ready to end it. I understood how difficult it was for Penelope to leave someone she loved—even if that person verbally abused or hit her. Even though she never asked for the abuse and wished she could erase it from her life completely, she had developed a bond over time with her boyfriend. And though the bond was not a healthy one, not every ounce of the bond is necessarily painful or destructive. In fact, abusers have moments when they can be soft and loving—and when victims are considering breaking the bond, remembering these moments can make them want to backpedal.

This is the trickiest part for the one being abused: Until she learns to redefine love, the tenderness and affection will always outweigh the mistreatment on the To-Dump-Him-Or-Not-to-Dump-Him Scale. The victim of the abuse must learn to see that although the good moments feel like love, *true love doesn't come in a package with abusive contents*. The hardest part for the victim involves understanding that what she thought of as love isn't really love at all. It's a bond that has developed over time—and that's not the same thing as love.

For Penelope, the breakthrough began here. She began to unearth the fact that there was something contaminated in her definition of love, in how she felt about herself, and in what she believed she deserved in a relationship. And although the breakthrough began at that point, we worked together for several more months on understanding how her behaviors made her a participant but not the holder of *all* responsibility in the abusive pattern. For Penelope, gaining insight into her motivations, into what she believed she deserved and what she expected from relationships, was a necessary first step in ensuring that she would never again find herself feeling trapped in an abusive relationship. Once she could recognize her self-destructive pattern of sacrificing herself for the sake of keeping the bond in her relationship alive, everything changed for Penelope.

THE TAKEAWAY

This chapter provided a glimpse into the catalysts that can bring about transformative moments on the road to real change. The women whose stories you've just read took the initiative to bring about change, which wasn't always easy or comfortable. Each one of them had the courage to stare reality in the face and look honestly at themselves and their own motivations in order to halt the vicious cycle of repetition. I always tell my clients to think about it this way: repeating destructive behavior is simply a form of drama. The cycle of repetition has a predictable script that will inevitably be read again and again until the RRs say "Enough!" and demand of themselves that the repetition be stopped dead in its tracks. You will come to see that assigning blame or focusing too much on your partners is a dead-end street, and that focusing on yourself and your behaviors—the only thing you can control—is how you will get the love life you're after.

Now that we have faced the first part of the model for change, let's look into why behaviors are equally as important as insight.

SELF-EVALUATION
Gaining Insight from Others' Experiences

1. Why do you think each of the women you've read about waited so long before they got help?

2. What attempts have you already made to change your repeating behavior?

3. Think about your last relationship and ask yourself, What were the earliest warning signs you saw that could have tipped you off to potential problems? How did you respond to those warning signs?

CHAPTER 8

Behavior Change

What Should Change Look Like?

IN THE LAST CHAPTER, we focused on the first key component of change: gaining insight. Now that you understand why insight, and the breakthrough of that "Aha!" moment, is a significant foundation for change, we are ready to move on to the behavioral component.

If you will, stop right here and do something for me. Take a deep breath. Now another. Later in the book, we'll talk about some helpful coping techniques that you can use both in your relationships and in your everyday life, but it doesn't hurt to try some of them now. A deep breath here and there can relieve some tension and prepare you to put on your hardhat and get to work!

The About-Face

Why is behavior change so important on the road to ousting problematic patterns? In a nutshell, behavior change is a must because insight alone—or knowing why you do something harmful—isn't enough. Insight must be followed by a concrete, observable change of some kind; maybe not as drastic as the sudden 180-degree turn a soldier makes when he or she does an about-face, but that's a good image to work with because that maneuver requires a definite posture change and affords a new perspective.

As we take a closer look at what goes into changing your relationship behavior, you'll see that it's within your control to choose how you behave. Will you choose behaviors that make you a participant in 1) repeating destructive patterns or 2) finding a new, fulfilling relationship? Together, let's shoot for the second option!

Because you've had a string of relationships that haven't worked for you, you've grown familiar with a set of behaviors that have had unproductive results. In other words, they don't make you happy because you don't end up with a lasting partner. Part of what I do with my clients who repeat toxic relationship patterns is determine where the problem behaviors start and then show the RR how to catch herself when she is tempted to re-enact old, unhealthy behaviors. In that moment, I show her how to redirect herself and switch into new behaviors that lead to healthier romantic outcomes. My goal here is to help you do the same. The process is not easy, and can bear jagged edges. You must have insight into yourself and your motivations so you can recognize the triggers that prompt you to engage in behaviors that keep you stuck on that hamster wheel of dysfunctional repetition.

As you read the following sections, take a close look at how the women introduced earlier in the book became hyperaware of their behaviors and eventually, sometimes after much struggle, replaced old behaviors with healthy ones.

Patricia

Patricia had her insight breakthrough when she realized that she needed to focus more on the emotional connection she had with a man than on certain other attributes, like how successful he was or how sexually attracted she felt to him. She learned that she must think about other compatibility issues, including whether their values overlapped and whether they liked the same kinds of people. Somewhere between completing the insight stage and finishing her work with me, Patricia's world was shaken up when she met a new man.

It was obvious from the start: Patricia had met someone who took her breath away. She shared details of their first few weeks together—the dinners they enjoyed and the weekend trip to the beach. He made her laugh, and she loved the fact that she liked his friends. She also felt reassurance because he was successful. He worked hard and she found that admirable. She felt herself falling fully head over heels until—and this came out of nowhere—she noticed something that upset her. Her new boyfriend, who initially seemed like the nicest guy, went on a nasty, jokey tirade about an overweight person who crossed the street in front of their car. Patricia was completely taken aback. He didn't seem to notice or care that she didn't laugh or respond.

As she got to know him a little better, this negative attitude and proclivity to make fun of others shone through more strongly. She openly admitted to herself and to me that she was totally turned off by the way he talked so hurtfully about complete strangers. It became apparent that he carried a bitter chip on his shoulder.

In a session with me, she voiced her frustration with that part of him and said it was so frustrating because "everything else about him was great." I suggested that Patricia stop right there for a moment and acknowledge the good news—she had become aware of these unappealing traits before she let herself fall deeply in love with him. While in the past she would have ignored the signs, focused instead on the one or two traits she felt were important, and then barreled full-speed ahead, her new insight forced her to be more aware of her relationships as they progressed step by step.

"What are you going to do with this information now?" I asked. Patricia sighed loudly and said she didn't know what to do. "Is this enough of a reason to break it off with someone?" she asked, with an anxious look on her face, hoping I'd come through with the easy response. I told her that the answer to that question had to come from her, and that she had to ask herself if she believed that her new boy-friend's values and her own were on the same page. After all, I told her, her past repeating was fueled by an overemphasis on external charac-teristics. I reminded her that we'd come to the conclusion that break-ing her bad-relationship cycle would only happen once she started focusing on her partner's internal characteristics, regardless of how successful or attractive he was.

A struggle followed for Patricia. She talked to her boyfriend and told him that she didn't think they were a good match, and that his mean streak cloaked in sarcasm had been eating at her. He was sur-prised and hurt, and that was it—they were officially done. However, the road to change wasn't smoothly paved. There were moments when she felt lonely and began to second-guess herself. "Sometimes I get so mad at myself, because I start feeling sure that I was just picking at something that really wasn't so bad. He never treated me badly," she confided. She admitted in a low voice that she had seen him again because she wasn't sure that the relationship should have ended.

I told Patricia that she was in the midst of a very natural struggle that follows attempts at change: the tendency to slip back into com-fortable old behaviors out of fear that the partner you really want won't ever come. Patricia's brief reunion with her ex-boyfriend was under-standable. After all, there was a lot about him that she liked. What she discovered, however, was that she needed to sit with the loneliness after a separation rather than act on her confused feelings. The next time he called, she told him that she was sorry and said she had to trust her instinct that they were not right for each other.

In this moment, when Patricia fully trusted her inner voice and newfound insight, she closed the door on him—and most important, on repeating. Rather than stick with the relationship and silence her instincts by pushing them under the rug, she gave him a firm "no" and closed the door. This behavior—identifying a problem and engaging in an alternative behavior to better protect herself—was new for her, and it sent a message loud and clear to the world, to herself, and to future partners: She knew what she wanted and she was done repeating. Patricia was moving on and burying that old tendency to repeat. She was through with settling.

Remember: Every step you take away from someone who isn't good for you is one step closer to someone who is.

Daphne

Integrating new behaviors into her life didn't come any easier for Daphne than it did for Patricia. Daphne was accustomed to her old ways, and it was a challenge for her to do things differently in her relationships. Looking back at how hard she tried, though, it makes sense that she was eventually able to figure it out for herself and move toward someone who made her happy.

It wasn't a new relationship that forced Daphne to change her ways and engage in new behaviors with men. It was an innocent-seeming hunk of metal and plastic: her cell phone. Every time she got frustrated or lonely, she was overwhelmed by a crippling urge to pick up the phone and call her ex-boyfriend Alex, who'd broken up with her after growing tired of her repeated questions about when they'd move in together. She knew her ill-advised calls were only keeping the residual drama alive with him, but she had difficulty restraining herself from the impulse to reach out to him. There were moments when she got stuck thinking about him and wondering what was going on his life, and those moments typically resulted in a phone call.

"I called him and I know that sounds bad," she told me honestly, after we had been talking about resisting urges to repeat her toxic relationship patterns. "The hard part is that it always makes me feel better to talk to him—to know he's there," she said. "Yes," I said, "but how do you feel a day or two afterward?" Daphne knew where I was going with this, and acknowledged that she felt better for a while but then always felt more depressed and lonely in the end. "Our job then,"

I said, "is to figure out what behaviors you can do in place of calling him when you know that he is not the boyfriend you ultimately want."

Daphne thought hard over the next couple of weeks, and we threw around different ideas. I tell my clients that you find what works by trial and error, and that's exactly how we went about strategizing her new behaviors. The hardest part for Daphne was getting through the moments when she was lonely or when she started feeling afraid that she would never meet and connect with anyone new, because that was when she felt the urge to contact her ex-boyfriend. Together, we figured out what comforted her most, and we used that to her advantage.

Similar to the way that Alcoholics Anonymous groups encourage all members to have a sponsor to call when they are in emotional need, we set up Daphne's best friend as her *repetition* sponsor. From that point on, each time she had the urge to contact her ex, she instead called her best friend, who calmed her down and sat with her through the uncomfortable feelings until, over time, they diminished. This was tough for Daphne, because she could be impulsive. However, Daphne showed progress as she agreed to sign on to this new strategy for change. She came to see the new behaviors as less desirable in the short term—because it's no fun sitting with anxiety and loneliness—but better for her in the long run.

Megan

You've gotten to know Megan's story fairly well by now. In reading about her experience with behavior change, you'll have the chance to see which behaviors she was forced to let go of and which ones she had to create from scratch. I probably don't need to remind you that Megan's Achilles' heel was men who were broken but who had enormous potential. In trying to fix them, she unconsciously hoped each time that her love—or what I would call her fixing—might strengthen her partner into the functional one she'd long hoped for.

"I'm confused about what I do now," she said. "I get that I need to understand why I do all these things I do in my relationships, but I don't get how I'm supposed to change into something else," she explained. Indeed, this is one of the hardest parts of the change process. Because you're not there yet and have functioned for so long the other way, you have no way of picturing how you can become something else—something better.

I shared with her one of my favorite expressions: "When you know better, you do better." I explained that *doing* better was all about paying attention to and altering behaviors, and that it was now time to change the way she approached emotionally broken men. After all, history had repeated itself long enough to prove that trying to have relationships with them simply wasn't going to work.

Megan and I figured out where the problem behaviors first set in— the precise moments, as she was getting to know a man, when his actions or confessions suggested that he might not be the best partner. She recalled that her last boyfriend had told her early on that his previous relationship had ended badly and that he "wanted to be good at being a boyfriend" but simply wasn't. She sensed at the time that he genuinely felt bad about this shortcoming, and that under all of his layers of complexity and self-doubt, he was a sweet guy with a lot of potential.

"Right there," I warned emphatically, "that's your cue for behavior change." I asked her how she responded at the time to him, and she said she reassured him that his assessment wasn't true. I leaned forward in my chair to be sure that she'd appreciate the importance of what I was about to say: "Megan, when a prospective partner tells you something about himself, believe him." I told her that the behavior change would require her, in that moment, to resist the urge to reassure the man and, instead, take the admission as a warning sign that he was not going to be a healthy romantic partner—for her or for anyone.

My suggestion elicited a scoff from Megan. "What?" she asked. "Just walk out of the restaurant because he was honest with me?" I told her that making good decisions didn't have to involve such extremes or drama, but that she had to recognize and accept the true significance of these signs—he wasn't a bad man, but likely a bad partner. I reminded her that dating isn't about assessing how good of a person someone is, but rather assessing how good of a boyfriend someone will be in the long term.

For Megan, making behavior changes to her usual repetition cycle meant that she had to avoid continuing relationships when her tendency was to stick them out and give her boyfriend chance after chance (after chance after chance) to change. Behavior change for Megan meant that she had to sit with feeling guilty or mean feelings with the next couple of men she dated as she figured out they weren't going to be suitable partners. "You're not mean," I told her, "but you do have a goal, and that goal is to find a long-term relationship that works. You have to remember that this is your life—not a game where you're just a plastic piece and there are no hurt feelings if you lose." As she continued the work, I witnessed the changes as she transformed into a woman who took herself and her life more seriously.

Penelope

Receipt of any form of abuse—whether physical, verbal, emotional, or neglect of any kind—can destroy a person's self-esteem and hope for a better future. Penelope had come to the realization in doing her insight work that all of her boyfriends had mistreated her in some way in the past, and had finally conceded that her current relationship wasn't fixable. At that point, we shifted our focus from gaining insight to changing her behaviors—a step I didn't anticipate would be easy.

Penelope was able to identify her feelings quickly and clearly. The toughest emotional moments for her in her relationship were the ones that came after the abuse—during the apology. During the moments when she was being verbally assaulted or even hit, she went into a shock-like state in which she felt numb, as if she weren't real or even there at all. This state of shock was her mind and body's way of protecting herself so that she could distance herself from the physical and emotional pain of the situation. Yet the period after the abuse, when her boyfriend sailed back in with his sweet and sorry act, was confusing and heart wrenching for her. Penelope was angry, but her emotions became quickly clouded. As soon as she would start packing her red suitcase, guilt would wash over her. In these moments, a voice inside told her that he wasn't evil and didn't deserve to be abandoned.

When her boyfriend laid on the syrupy apology, Penelope typically withdrew behind a stoic façade and told him in a rational voice that he couldn't keep doing that to her. It made the situation even more emotionally conflicting for her when he would try to hold her or make a warm sexual overture. It wasn't an act—he did love her in his own inconsistent, twisted way. Further, because she had been starving for that sweet side, her resolve would crumble and she'd give in to his touch in order to reconnect with him emotionally. The abuse had caused an underlying desperation to get back to a place that felt more loving.

"I know everyone tells me to leave him, but that sounds too simple," she said. "It's not that easy when you've built a whole life together," she added, as if trying to convince me. "To give up after trying so damn hard seems even crazier," she said. "I'm waiting for the payoff—the good—after putting up with the bad for so long," Penelope said.

There, sitting on my couch, Penelope wore the most exhausted expression. On her face, I could see what years of waiting and sacrificing looked like. "I can't pull you out of the relationship—only you can do that if you choose to in the end," I told her in one session. "I believe mistreatment or abuse can be a life-or-death issue, so I have to encourage anyone in such a relationship to leave," I warned. "However, if you choose to stay at this point, you must be willing to concede *something*: You have to change some of your behaviors because things can't continue as they are."

Penelope knew how bad the circumstances had become. She was no dummy, and she'd spent a lot of time and energy surviving her various romantic relationships, so we both knew there was a vast reserve of strength inside her. "What can you do the next time he mistreats you in any way?" I asked. "Leave the situation—that's what I always do," she said. "What do you do later?" I asked, and she replied, "I come back to see if he's cooled down."

"Penelope," I explained, "you are not guilty of being hit. You aren't the one getting physically aggressive or making the verbal attacks." I told her that what she needed to do to break the repetition cycle was to determine which behaviors she engaged in that reinforced the cycle of abuse. "Maybe what you need to do after an incident of mistreatment is to stay away a little longer," I said. "By now," I explained, "he has gotten it in his head that no matter what you say, he can do this to you because he knows you will keep coming back."

The truth was, Penelope didn't simply come back because she wanted to check on her boyfriend and see what his emotional state was. Yes, she hoped that he had cooled down, but separating from him after the abuse was also very painful. In these moments, she sought reconnection to feel better. She felt alone during the abusive episode, and then being without her boyfriend made it even harder. Women in healthy relationships turn to their boyfriends when something distressing happens. But where are abused women supposed to turn when they are mistreated? Paradoxically, the one they want to turn to is the very one they need to avoid.

Penelope's return to the house after the abusive outburst was one of the behaviors that needed to change. And once she had returned, her acceptance of her boyfriend's warm embrace or apology was the other behavior that she'd have to give up. If she wasn't prepared to leave him, she had to start somewhere—she had to put her old behaviors on notice and begin the process of inviting new ones to take their place.

The session after our intense conversation about what to do next, she told me about an incident that had taken place three nights before. She was shaken, but she said she'd surprised herself by how firm she'd been with him.

Penelope had been putting on her makeup and was soon to be on her way out of the apartment for a night with her girlfriends. As her friends waited in the living room for her to finish getting ready, he pulled her into the bedroom. So her friends couldn't hear, he hissed into her ear that she was dressing like a "dirty whore," and pushed her down onto the bed, demanding that she change her clothing.

By this point, Penelope knew that her behavior had to change in order for anything else to change. We had already addressed how to focus on behavior change: 1) to address it in the instant that it occurred and 2) to not return home as if nothing had happened.

Immediately after her boyfriend issued his derogatory slur, she sat up and said to him, "You can't treat me like this, because I won't tolerate it." It didn't even matter how he responded—the point was that she needed to say it out loud so that she could hear herself say it and then actually start to believe it. After she left the apartment, she engaged in her second behavioral change: she stayed away a little longer than she would have in the past. In fact, she didn't come home that night at all, or the next day. She had more than her fill of messages from Lawrence on her voice mail, first angry and then those that took on a sad, desperate tone. In those later messages, he pleaded for her to come back.

Listening to her boyfriend sound so desperate broke her heart. In fact, he seemed to feel the same way she felt when he hurt her, which actually made her feel closer to him. "When he's soft like that," she said, "that's when I love him the most—he's such a softie underneath it all." Though I disagreed with her, I told her that whether he was truly a "softie" was something she could determine in the future, after she had done more work to change how she operated in the relationship.

The behaviors Penelope needed to change—or the ones she was willing to work on—included going back to him too soon after the upsetting event and accepting his attempts to reach out to her when he was desperate and pleading. Changing her behavior—learning to do something different in the face of the same old triggers—was harder than she'd ever dreamed, but somehow, not impossible!

In the next chapter, when we focus on the end result of this work, we will talk about how your identity can start to change for the better. The courage and resilience Penelope showed on the road to changing her identity will remind you that we all, deep down, have the potential for change inside of us—it's simply a matter of making a resolute decision to say "enough is enough."

THE TAKEAWAY

The second stage of change—targeting the behaviors that hold you back and replacing them with new ones—brought the RRs you've read about one giant step closer to a better relationship. RRs have become so accustomed to responding in a habitual way to their partners that they lose touch with the fact that they are actually reinforcing the repetition cycle. The women whose stories you just finished were not always ready at first to respond in the way that I suggested. Changing behaviors can make you feel lonely or disoriented—like arriving home in the evening to find the layout of your house completely rearranged. Just as you wouldn't know quite how to find your way to your old room, the RRs can feel overwhelmed by how unfamiliar and uncomfortable the new behaviors feel. But we'll soon see how the RRs had to sit with the feelings that followed their new behaviors in order to reach the brass ring that follows—identity change.

SELF-EVALUATION
Are You Ready to Change?

1. As you read the stories from this chapter, whose story spoke to you the most? With whom could you best relate?

2. What behaviors would be hardest for you to change when it comes to responding to the old type of man you are attracted to?

3. What feelings will be the most difficult for you to sit with as you soon start to change your own behaviors?

CHAPTER 9

Identity Change

A New Perspective on You

WHEN YOU'RE WORKING TOWARD a goal, it's necessary on occasion to get a sense that you're getting one step closer to the big payoff. We're getting closer to the final stage of our prescription for change. This final stage focuses on identity and how it begins to evolve as a result of working through the first stage (insight) and second stage (behavior change).

This chapter will provide you with a big-picture look at the women you've been reading about, one that allows you to see how their awareness and behavior changes actually caused a shift in the way they saw themselves and the way they approached romantic relationships. As soon as we finish rounding out the circle of change for these women, we'll dive into your life in the next chapter!

The Payoff

When we first looked at the model for change, I explained that the insight stage is characterized by the breakthrough: that moment when you feel a mental click as you uncover the patterns in your behavior and the motivations that underlie it. Following that, the behavior change stage is characterized by catching yourself when you're triggered to fall back into old behaviors and doing something different instead. The third and final stage—identity change—is where you reap the fruits of your labor.

In the identity change stage, recovering RRs get what I call the payoff. By the time you get here, you've done the work and now begin to see examples of how you're changing for the better. After gaining insight and changing your behaviors, you begin to notice how your identity—the way you see yourself and your relationships—is taking the shape of one that's stronger and healthier. Here, you'll see the payoff in the lives of the RRs we've followed throughout their transformation.

Patricia

The journey toward change was not easy for Patricia, but she was gradually learning that she needed to prize the internal characteristics of her partners more than the external ones—regardless of how attractive or successful the men were. She finally accepted that the emotional connection shared with her partner, as well as his values and kindness, were the critical ingredients in a worthwhile relationship.

Patricia trudged through the "dirty work," as I call it, which involves becoming aware of your motivations and sitting with all the uncomfortable feelings that come with not yet having proof that a better relationship awaits you. But all of her hard work rewarded her in the end. In the final stage of her recovery from the repetition cycle, she was dumbfounded by how differently she experienced the new dating situations she found herself in.

"I went out with this guy recently, and I felt like I was practically interviewing him for a job," she said with a grin. "I'm kind of surprised I didn't bring a clipboard with me and take notes," she laughed. "After all this talking and thinking about who I'm attracted to, I can't even really understand how I ever fell for a man based on a chiseled face and a good suit," she said confidently.

For Patricia, changing her identity meant that she had begun to approach new romantic relationships in an entirely different way than she had in the past. For one thing, she now approached a first date hoping to meet a friend (and possibly more), rather than wishing this date would end up being The One. By approaching her dates in this manner, she took the pressure off herself so she could relax and actually have an open, honest exchange with a new man. Second, she asked the men she dated a lot of questions and was careful in listening to what they had to say. She wasn't testing them, but there was a reality she now faced—she needed to know whether her dates had brought a set of puzzle pieces to the table that fit with hers.

One of the most significant changes I noticed in Patricia's new relationship identity had to do with her time frame. In the past, Patricia always felt compelled to determine instantly whether she felt attracted to a man. While in the past she had been quick to idealize the men she was interested in, she now had to figure out when to put on the brakes and slow down. Patricia learned to take her time and remind herself that there was no rush—she didn't have to make any immediate decisions. She could take a few months and get to know someone before she let herself fully fall for him—and this was an entirely new experience for her. She had no idea that she could have so much control over herself in her romantic relationships—and what sweet relief this was!

Patricia's Takeaway

Following the model for change allowed Patricia to slow down and ease into a relationship. Because the new relationship identity she created was a cautious one, she could now guarantee that she wouldn't simply repeat any patterns on autopilot or find herself deep in a relationship without making sure she felt good about the partner she chose. What's more, slowing down and looking at all of the characteristics of a man allowed her to stop idealizing and start seeing the whole person. After all, it's a whole person you have to mesh with in a long-term relationship. I often use a metaphor with my clients that they find helpful. If you were going to take $10,000 and invest it in the stock market, you wouldn't simply pour your hard-earned money into the first company you heard about. You would look at several stocks simultaneously, watch the stock price over a period of time, and ask a few friends or colleagues what their thoughts were about the investment. If you take that kind of care with your money, isn't it time that you take equivalent (or greater!) care with your heart?

Daphne

For RRs who have spent years emotionally chasing unavailable partners, the payoff couldn't come a day too soon. Daphne, for example, had begun the journey toward change and was shocked when she started to see her hard work pay off. After so much time spent settling for men who gave her what I call "less-than-love" and feeling pushed away in some way or other, the final stage of recovery from the repetition cycle brought her peace of mind and renewed her faith in the future.

The cell phone and the urge to reach out to an old boyfriend who had left her high and dry symbolized the behavior change Daphne had to master. Though calling him meant putting herself in a vulnerable position, she previously told herself the risk was worth it as long as the reconnection soothed her sadness and loneliness, even if it was only temporary.

Daphne learned to sit with the discomfort and trudge through the lonely feelings. In doing so, Daphne faced her fears. She realized that the bad feelings eventually pass and give rise to better ones. What's more, she came to see that sitting with her feelings—as opposed to always acting out on them—ultimately raised her self-esteem.

"A week or so ago, it got really bad and I almost called him," she said, referring to reaching out to the ex-boyfriend who never wanted to fully commit to her. "But I started to think—for what? What would it really change?" Daphne rearranged herself on the sofa and sat up straight as she said defiantly, "I gave him more than enough chances and he blew each and every one of them."

I smiled. Daphne's new identity was taking shape.

Daphne's Takeaway

Daphne had spent so long focusing on her boyfriend's thoughts and feelings that she'd completely neglected her own. However, as she worked through the insight and behavior change stages, she got in touch with the anger and frustration she felt after chasing someone for so long who proved eternally unavailable. Daphne finally reached the stage of identity change when she came to see herself as someone who was capable of having a more meaningful relationship and who deserved better—not pitiful excuses and put-offs.

Megan

Over time, rescuing wounded souls gets old—very old. One of the most fascinating things about recovery from this repeated pattern is how hard it is to change in the beginning. Another is how fast change comes following the first hurdle. Though the rescuer spends years bending over backward and tolerating everything, once the RR begins to give up the role of rescuer, all undue tolerance tends to disappear and the pendulum often swings dramatically in the other direction. Megan was no exception.

Having invested many years of her life loving men who she believed had "tons of potential" but even more emotional baggage, Megan set off down the road toward change and didn't look back for long. She worked on her insight and behavior change stages with earnest diligence, uncovering the ugly realities of years surrendered to lost romantic causes and engaging in new behaviors when she faced her old emotional triggers. After all of her hard work, she experienced the payoff in unexpected ways.

Once Megan began working my program of change, she did things differently with men. For the first time in her life, she forced herself to stay single and avoided dating altogether for six months. This experience was unusual for Megan because she'd been accustomed to constant attachment to a man. Megan took a romantic hiatus so that she could make sure she was emotionally sober before she let herself fall for someone new.

During the period that Megan was alone, it wasn't all bubble baths and contented sighs over glasses of Cabernet. In truth, this period presented Megan with many uncomfortable first-time experiences, like going to parties by herself. When people asked her if she had a boyfriend, she initially responded "No," with a quick explanation to defend her single status. On a couple of occasions, she caught herself saying "but that's out of choice—I want to be single." Over time, she found that she didn't need to explain herself to anyone. Family and friends could encourage her to date all they wanted, but what mattered was what *she* wanted. For the first time in her life, she was beginning to put herself first. She made a conscious decision to say that her self-worth had nothing to do with a man—whether being with him or fixing him.

After several months of being alone, Megan began to wade gently into dating waters, but she did so at a careful pace. When she met a man she found attractive, she forced herself to take inventory of what traits appealed to her. She found herself repeating a mantra in her head as she got to know the new man she was dating: If he never changed, would I be okay with him as a husband? At the very beginning, she questioned whether she could be attracted to someone who had it all together—this was a whole new ball game for her. Over time, however, she realized that it didn't always have to be so black-and-white.

"At first, with Jason, he seemed like he had everything so together, that he almost wouldn't even need me," she confided as she told me about a new man she'd been seeing. "But soon after," she said, "it hit me that being needed so early in a relationship is actually a bad sign." I reminded her again and again, "Remember, you'll be happy when you get to be a girlfriend, not a therapist." I joked that therapy was my job and that she shouldn't feel like she is always working when she returns home to a man. Megan breathed a sigh of relief and continued to fill me in on the changes she had been noticing in her interactions with men. She wore a peaceful expression for the first time in months.

Megan's Takeaway

After spending so many lost hours of her life trying to understand, figure out, and fix the men she loved, Megan finally learned what it felt like to simply love a man as is. When she let herself fall for someone who was emotionally strong and stable, she could finally give up the role of mommy-therapist and audition for the sought-after role of girlfriend. This shift revolutionized her romantic identity and the way she saw herself in her life. She finally learned that what she thought of as love wasn't really love, after all—it was pity and caretaking. Megan could finally move on once she learned the difference.

Penelope

In a nutshell, the change for Penelope was drastic. She had experienced the pattern of mistreatment—and in some cases, abuse—at the hands of multiple boyfriends, and finally began to turn a blind eye to her current boyfriend's all-too-predictable sweet song-and-dance following a hurtful or abusive episode. In the beginning of this work—and I do mean work—changing her reactions was challenging. Like a new shoe that causes pain, the new behaviors were not worn easily or comfortably. However, just as a new shoe begins to conform to the foot and not fight it after a period of wear, Penelope found that the new behaviors fit a little more comfortably once she committed and gave them a real chance.

Penelope noticed the most significant change in herself following the episode when she was getting ready to go out with her girlfriends and her boyfriend threw her down on the bed, refusing to let her go until she changed her clothes. After she initiated a behavior that acted as a significant consequence to his abuse—staying away for a couple of days and refusing his warm attempts to reconnect and apologize later—Penelope noticed a surprising difference: She was *still* angry.

In the past, she reluctantly received his apologies and advances, which served to lessen or even erase her anger. At the time, she didn't realize she was making herself a complicit partner in an abusive relationship and that her efforts to survive him were actually reinforcing his behavior.

WHEN SEX IS DESTRUCTIVE

Sex can be a transformative emotional experience in that it can drastically take you out of one feeling and propel you into feelings that are totally different. If you feel sad one moment, for example, sex can take you to another emotional place almost instantly—ecstatic, vulnerable, and the list goes on.

I always tell my clients to take note of their feelings when they begin to have sex with their partners. I encourage them to ask themselves if they feel happy or sad, excited or angry prior to the sexual experience. It's an important pattern to look out for, because sometimes RRs look to sex to fix or heal emotional problems. In this way, sex can provide a temporary fix but ultimately reinforce dysfunctional dynamics in their relationships.

Penelope implemented some serious consequences after the last abusive episode. Because we established the fact that her repeated pattern meant that she sacrificed herself in her relationships, we made a priority of doing the opposite from that point on. Rather than sacrifice herself and her feelings, she started to put herself first and demand that things change in her relationship.

"Honestly, he was shocked that I didn't come home for two days," she said. She folded her arms across her chest and added, "And I was a little surprised by myself, too." Penelope looked me straight in the face and said, "I didn't know, at first, if I could do it, but once I did, that was *it*. It's like someone else inside me took over, and I just refused to be that same girl." Penelope had taken a gigantic step in putting a stop to her old dysfunctional and repetitive pattern. "Penelope, it wasn't someone else inside you—it was all the feelings you had stuffed down that you recently learned to bring to the surface," I assured her. "You finally decided that you are in total control of yourself and that you weren't born to waste away in an abusive relationship."

The identity change stage for Penelope introduced her to the old Penelope that she'd thrown under the rug for many years—the one who was innocent and loving, hopeful and emotionally hungry. After years of putting up with less-than-love, she believed that this type of self-sacrificing love was all that she could get or all that she deserved in this lifetime. The verbal attacks and physical hits had hurled massive blows to her identity, manipulating her into believing that this was as a good as it gets. However, once she gained insight into the dynamic between herself and her boyfriend and started to change her behaviors in the relationship, the changes in her identity followed. In the end, the goal wasn't to change her boyfriend; it was to change herself—because Penelope was the one who needed to walk out of that relationship.

"I left him," Penelope said quietly. "I was a fool to think it would change, because it happened one more time," she said. "But when he did it the next time, I just never went back. The time that I stayed away for a couple of days changed me—I realized I could live without him. Yes, I'm sad that I'm without him, but I felt alone anyway for so much of that relationship," she said as she reflected on the months of confusion and anxiety she felt. "I just realized I'd rather be alone than put myself in that kind of situation again."

Penelope's Takeaway

Change for Penelope was bittersweet. While some RRs forgo the old partners for better ones, and some manage to do so fairly quickly, identity change isn't always so instant and rosy for others. The shift for Penelope meant that she gave up the identity of a victim and sacrificer, and learned to try on a whole new kind of shoe—one that she had not worn in ages. Leaving her boyfriend resulted in a period in which she felt sadness and loneliness, but it also meant that she had the chance to feel other feelings, too—self-respect and self-love, self-protection, and hope for the future. Most of all, she learned to see herself as someone who deserved more than a bond—she deserved real love. In the end, she was able to stop seeing herself as a victim and to start seeing herself as a navigator—a woman who navigates her own course in this world in a way that leads to self-protection and the realization of the goals she has for her life.

THE TAKEAWAY

In this chapter, we discussed the third and final stage of the model for change—identity change. The chapter allowed you to gain a more full perspective of what change truly looks like, and how you can reach the payoff by engaging in all the hard work of the insight and behavior change stages. Although you have followed these women on their paths toward change and have seen the differences, you have probably also picked up on the similarities in their stories. In one way or other, each RR is settling and automatically repeating a toxic pattern because her identity tells her this is what she is supposed to do. I'm here to tell you that the script is far from finished! We are now going to turn our attention to you and your life, your pattern, and your partners. The next part of the book will require you to pick up a pen and fill in the following pages, digging deep into your memories, thoughts, feelings, and wishes. Congratulations for making it this far. Now we can rewrite your script so that it has a happier ending!

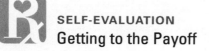

SELF-EVALUATION

Getting to the Payoff

1. How would you describe the payoff as it relates to your own life? Write down your answer in the journal you are keeping as you read this book.

2. At this stage, before you complete your Insight Inventories, what do you think is keeping you from your payoff? What reality might you be fighting? What behavior might you need to try to reach your payoff?

3. From where you sit right now, what do you think your identity tells you to expect from your romantic relationships?

PART III

Hands-On Insight
Inventories

CHAPTER 10

Your Story

What Makes You Tick?

AS YOU BEGIN THIS section, take a moment to glance into your rearview mirror and note how much distance you've already covered. When it comes to changing the way you think about relationships and breaking the repetition cycle, you're farther than you've ever been before.

Up to this point, we have focused on the four commonly repeated patterns, as well as the stories of women who repeated them. This focus serves to remind you that 1) you are not alone in your experience with men, and 2) change is, in fact, possible. The stage has been set so that we can now turn the camera on you.

We'll start by breaking down your story into three parts: your personality, your core beliefs about yourself, and your overall decision-making style. Each part will include its own exercises, all designed to be interesting and fun—or as much fun as working on relationships can be! The exercises will require you to fill out some simple questionnaires and engage in a few visualization exercises.

I call the exercises in this chapter Insight Inventories because, again, gaining insight is the first step of my prescription for change. People who know themselves well can take better care of themselves and have less risk of losing themselves in a relationship or repeating toxic relationship patterns. As the goal of this book is to break the cycle of RRS and to stop repeating, it may seem obvious to start by focusing on your relationships. However, RRs often repeat their respective patterns because they are out of touch with themselves in some critical way. Therefore, the first part of the journey toward recovery is to focus on yourself. In turn, the first thing you must do to focus on yourself is to identify your interests, hobbies, values, and fantasies. Once you have identified these factors, you can figure out what your true needs are.

Personality: The Essence of Who You Are

Everyone has heard the terms "introverted" and "extroverted." Do you know which you are? Before answering this question, let me first address the myth that applies to how people understand these terms. Whether someone is an introvert or extrovert is not about how social or timid someone is. It is actually about how people meet their primary emotional needs: from within (introvert) or from others (extrovert).

When your energy is low and your internal resources are depleted, you need to recharge your batteries. Introverts need time alone or a solitary activity to recharge their batteries. In a nutshell, they go internally to refuel. Extroverts often seek the company of others, meaning that it is from social interaction that they refuel. When their energy is low, they come alive in the context of social interaction.

Whether you are an introvert or extrovert is one of the most fundamental aspects of your personality. As you work through the following exercise, ask yourself which personality type—introverted or extroverted—best fits you.

EXERCISE: Your Personality, Values, and Interests

Here, you'll find several categories and questions within each category. The categories are made up of some of the central components of our lives, including work, family, and play. Beside each question, assign a number using a simple scale of 1 to 10, in which 1 is "not at all" and 10 is "totally or as much as possible."

Social

1. How social are you, in general? _____

2. How much do you like to attend social functions where you may run into friends, family, or neighbors? _____

3. How frequently do you like to visit with your friends during the week or the weekend? _____

4. How much do you like alone time? _____

Religiosity

1. How religious or spiritual are you? _____

2. How much do you practice this religion or spirituality in or out of the house? _____

Hobbies

1. How important are your hobbies in your weekly routine? _____

2. How much do you read or engage in other solitary quiet activities (e.g., knitting, doing crossword puzzles, etc.)? _____

3. How much time do you spend watching television? _____

4. How much do you enjoy watching or engaging in athletic activities? _____

Drugs and Alcohol

1. How often do you drink alcohol? _____

2. How much do you use drugs (e.g., marijuana, others)? _____

3. How important is to you that you be able to engage in this behavior in a relationship? _____

Relationship with Family of Origin (family you were born into)

1. How important is your family to you? _____

2. How much contact would you like to have with your family? _____

3. How much contact do you actually have with your family? _____

Stability

1. How stable are your moods? _____

2. How stable are your finances? _____

3. How stable are your friendships? _____

Work

1. How passionately do you feel about the kind of work that you do?

    _____

2. If you are a stay-at-home mother or father, how much do you enjoy staying home with the children? _____

3. How much of your day do you spend doing the kind of work that you do? _____

4. How much of your weekend do you spend thinking about or doing work? _____

Physical Affection

1. How physically affectionate are you with your friends and lovers (e.g., holding hands, holding an arm, rubbing someone's back)?

   _____

2. How comfortable are you engaging in mild public displays of affection (e.g., holding hands)? _____

Verbally Expressive

1. How often do you talk about your negative feelings (e.g., sadness, anger, loneliness)? _____

2. How comfortable are you confronting someone with whom you are angry? _____

3. How comfortable are you asking someone for help with a task?

   _____

Sex

1. How sexual are you, in general? _____

2. How frequently do you like to have sex in your relationships? _____

3. How comfortable are you with your body? _____

Marriage

1. How important is it to you to get married? _____

2. How important is the type of ceremony you have? _____

Children

1. How important is it to you to have children? _____

2. How important is the number of children you have? _____

3. How important is it to you to have your own biological children?

   _____

Pets

1. How important is it to you to have pets? _____

2. How important is the number and type of pets that you have?

   _____

Now that you have completed this list, we are going to look at your responses on a few levels. There is no right or wrong way to answer the questions or to interpret your responses.

Task A

Look at the items where you gave a response of 8 or higher and 2 or lower. Responses with these scores are important because they fall at the far ends of the spectrum and, as a result, tell you a lot about yourself. Responses at the extreme end indicate that you feel strongly about these areas. For these responses, circle the item so that you can take special note of its importance to you. Questions to consider:

1. Did you already know that you felt strongly about these areas?

   _____

2. Did you express these values or interests of yours openly to your last partner?

_____

3. If you have several or more responses that are 2 or lower or 8 or higher, what does this mean about you?

_____

4. Are you more inclined to think it means that you are headstrong and overly opinionated, or that you know yourself well and know what you want?

_____

Task B

Look at each item where you responded with a 5. These responses mean that you do not feel strongly about this issue. Questions to consider:

1. Did you know that you were lukewarm to these issues?

_____

2. Did you express to your last partner that these particular areas were not particularly important to you?

_____

It's fairly obvious to point out that our extreme responses tell us the things we feel strongly about, but let's clarify what a response in the middle indicates. When we don't feel strongly one way or another about something, it suggests that we can be neutral about some issues and do not extend opinions on every subject unless we feel strongly about it.

1. If you have several or more responses of 5, what does this mean about you?

_____

_____

_____

2. Do you think that several responses of 5 indicate that you are malleable and look to others to define how you feel about things? Conversely, do you think that they indicate that you are easygoing and flexible, and open to many different possibilities?

_____

_____

_____

Dr. Seth's Personality Exercises: Unique But Effective

Now that you have considered your general personality style, interests, and values, we are going to engage in some exercises that will help you to more clearly define your personality. In this section I have included a few exercises that I've developed, some of which may seem unusual but which are highly effective at identifying your personality traits. Although they have not been tested in an official research setting, they are exercises that I have used with clients and that clients have found incredibly useful.

THE WINDOW TECHNIQUE: A Personality Visualization

As part of my doctoral training in clinical psychology, I learned how to administer and conduct a wide range of psychological tests. Among them, I studied the Rorschach Inkblot Test, otherwise known simply as the inkblot test, which you may have seen or heard about at some point throughout your life.

In my final year of graduate school, I taught a testing lab of first-year doctoral students and reviewed with them the complex interpretation of the inkblot test. The complexity of the variables involved in the test's interpretation is astonishing. In training the students how to interpret the test, I noticed that the students were not capturing the essences of the patients they were testing. The students had the tendency to get lost in the jargon as they wrote their interpretation reports, and they lost sight of the patients' overall personalities.

Ultimately, I had the most success in helping the students to paint a three-dimensional picture of a patient when I asked them to employ a tactic I call the Window Technique. To encourage them to flesh out their impressions of the personalities they were working with, I told my students to ask themselves the following questions about their patients. For the purposes of this exercise, these same questions are directed at you.

1. If someone looked at you through a window and saw you in a room with someone, what might you be doing?

   _____

2. What might this window observer guess your mood is like? Would you likely be laughing and smiling, or appear depressed and angry? Would you be moving about or sitting still?

   _____

3. If someone looking through the window were to x-ray your brain and find out what you were thinking, what is an example of a thought you'd likely be thinking?

   _____

4. If the person looking through the window were asked how happy or fulfilled you were overall in your life, what might this person say?

   _____

FAVORITE FILMS: A Cinematic Personality Exercise

Another fun way to determine your personality style is to think about the films you like and why you like them. Some films are plot-driven (for example, action films), and others are more character-driven (that is, focusing on the characters and dialogue). Plot-driven films tend to have a greater focus on what is going on, while character-driven films tend to focus more on the personalities involved. An example of a popular plot-driven film is *The Matrix*, while an example of a popular character-driven film is *Sex and the City*.

Ask yourself the following questions about the films you like.

1. Which films do you prefer: plot-driven or character-driven?

    _____

2. What are three of your favorite films? Why are they your favorites?

    _____

3. Don't think about this next question too long: Who are the first couple of characters from movies that pop into your head? Why do you think these characters stick out in your mind?

    _____

4. After watching a film for the first time, how much time do you like to spend talking about it with the person you saw it with (on average):

    A minute or so _____
    About five minutes _____
    Ten minutes or longer _____

These questions will tell you a lot about your personality. If you only like plot-driven movies and you don't want to talk about the film afterward, it may mean that you feel more comfortable focusing on concrete observations and what is immediately visible on the surface, rather than going deeper and talking about thoughts or feelings. On the other hand, if your responses suggest that you love dramas and enjoy talking about the film's characters over dessert afterward, it could ultimately indicate that you like to analyze and to discuss ideas and events in depth. Regardless of what your responses were, they can tell you a lot about your personality.

THE TWO SIDES OF PERSONALITY: A Small-Screen

The next exercise is similar to the one you just finished, but it is more specific than the last one. Before we jump into it, I will give you some background on how I created this exercise. Most of my family, friends, and colleagues joke that I am the archetypal psychologist—always deconstructing and analyzing. They joke that analysis is both work and a hobby for me. As evidence of the reality behind this joke, I confess that one of my favorite questions to ask someone upon meeting them is who their favorite character was on the popular television show *The Golden Girls*.

Looking at *The Golden Girls* through an analytical lens is helpful in illuminating what I call the two sides of our respective personalities. People are complicated and can't be reduced to one simple personality trait. Each of us has a number of traits, many of them seemingly contradictory. I believe that each person has a general presentation— the way she or he comes across to others who don't know them well; and a more hidden side—one that requires mutual trust and a lot of time before it reveals itself. In terms of the characters on *The Golden Girls*, I believe it is a testament to the show's writers and actors that my informal poll over the years has elicited such a strong and immediate response from my audience. People, I believe, respond in this way because they like and/or identify on a basic personality level with the characters: Dorothy, Sophia, Rose, and Blanche.

The show's characters are memorable because of the way they were drawn. Each character has two sides, which adds to the complexity of the characters' personalities: all four women have an overt side and a covert side. For instance, when Dorothy's overt side is on display, she's outspoken and fearless, but her covert side indicates that she is shy and somewhat awkward with men. Sophia's overt side has a sharp-tongued and no-nonsense demeanor, but her covert side indicates that she is a pussycat sentimentalist when it comes to the true love she has for her daughter. Rose's overt side is spacey and foolish, but her covert side reveals a down-to-earth nature and wisdom when least expected. Finally, Blanche's overt side is sex-obsessed and vain, but her covert side indicates that she is warm and deeply loyal to those close to her.

Sex and the City is another show that portrays the different sides of its characters. Carrie, for example, likes to present herself as extremely confident and independent, but her covert side indicates that she can become overly dependent on a man (I'm sure if you've watched the show or movies you can think of one Big example of what I mean) to make her happy. Similarly, Samantha's overt side indicates that she is wild and promiscuous, though her covert side indicates that she can be vulnerable and sweet when she lets her guard down, and that she has some doubts about her fiercely independent lifestyle. While Charlotte's overt side presents a one-note, Pollyanna-ish attitude, her covert side indicates that she is also adventurous and curious underneath that façade. Finally, Miranda's overt side suggests that she is overly career-driven and sarcastic, and at times a bit cold, but beneath that surface she has an almost tenacious drive to show warmth and affection to her inner circle.

The important point about these characters is that each has two sides, like many of us do in our lives. Each character has an overt side that acts as almost like a defense mechanism, a steel veneer that protects against the most vulnerable and authentic part of each character's authentic personality. I believe you will find the analysis of these characters useful in considering your own personality style. The following are some questions to consider.

1. Who is your favorite *Golden Girl* or *Sex and the City* character and why?

    _____

2. Did you choose your favorite because you consider yourself to be like her or because you wish you could be more like her?

    _____

3. How would you describe your overt side? What about your covert side?

    _____

4. Do you present one persona but have another side most people don't see?

    _____

Core Beliefs: The Beliefs You Hold about Yourself

In taking inventory of why you repeat toxic relationship patterns, we must consider one possible motivator for your behavior. When it comes to psychology and the laws of human behavior, we have to accept that there are many questions to which we don't yet know the answers. After working for years in clinics with schizophrenic patients, I am still shocked that we don't know why people are schizophrenic—all we have are unproven theories. In consideration of why you repeat dysfunctional relationship patterns, we are going to take another brief look at researcher Judith Beck's core beliefs theory.

Essentially, Beck's theory says that people's most deeply held beliefs are what influence their feelings. She has determined that most peoples' core beliefs are rooted in one of two negative core beliefs: helplessness or worthlessness.

In her book *Cognitive Therapy*, Beck defined the two categories of beliefs with the following examples.

HELPLESS CORE BELIEFS

- I am helpless.
- I am powerless.
- I am out of control.
- I am weak.
- I am vulnerable.
- I am needy.
- I am trapped.
- I am inadequate.
- I am ineffective.
- I am incompetent.
- I am a failure.
- I am disrespected.
- I am defective (i.e., I do not measure up to others).
- I am not good enough (in terms of achievement).

Unlovable Core Beliefs

- I am unlovable.
- I am unlikable.
- I am undesirable.
- I am unattractive.
- I am unwanted.
- I am uncared for.
- I am bad.
- I am unworthy.
- I am different.
- I am defective (i.e., so others will not love me).
- I am not good enough (to be loved by others).
- I am bound to be rejected.
- I am bound to be abandoned.
- I am bound to be alone.

Read through this list again, circling any that apply to how you feel in day-to-day life, not on how you feel at this moment. In general, when you are upset, what do you feel? What do you think? What is the inner dialogue that you say to yourself?

If you repeat relationships, you can probably relate to at least one of these core beliefs.

No, it is not easy or fun to acknowledge unpleasant realties, but it is a crucial part of breaking the repetition cycle. You must strive to be honest with yourself and admit the truth, so that you can learn how to move on. Once you face the things you are most afraid of, you can look back and see that what scared you originally isn't so scary after all. In other words, often the idea or fear of something is scarier than the real thing!

Take a look at these questions and answer them without thinking too much about them. Remember, there are no correct answers!

1. Of the items that you circled in the lists of core beliefs, write the two items that fit you best on the lines below.

   _____

2. How might these feelings have impacted whom you sought for a partner in the past?

   _____

3. How might these feelings have impacted why you stayed in a relationship even though you'd become unhappy in it?

   _____

Decision-Making Style: How You Make Decisions

The topic of decision-making may not seem like a topic related to romantic repetition. However, when you stop to consider that you're putting your decision-making skills to use every time you choose which partner to start dating, it becomes apparent that your decision-making skills are incredibly important—even central to this discussion. The concept that making good decisions reflects actual skill might be one you never considered before. After finishing this section and, ultimately, this book, you will know exactly what this means.

One of the most consistent patterns I've found in working with women who repeat toxic relationship patterns is that they often speak about their poor relationships as if the relationships simply "happened" to them. Relationships do not simply happen to you; you play an active role in seeking them out. You are an active participant. Seeing the issue any other way enables the dysfunction—it lets you off the hook to suggest that someone other than you was responsible for your behavior.

Looking back at any relationship, the first decision you made was to agree to participate in a conversation, and the rest followed from that first decision. Countless other decisions followed. Why might a person want to believe that a bad relationship happened to her? *Because she doesn't want to own the fact that she half-created a bad relationship.*

There are two ways of looking at your relationships:

They happen to you

versus

You seek them out

It's important to avoid overthinking things, because it's actually very simple: Even if you don't initiate relationship interactions, as long as you're standing there next to that person, you become an active participant in *continuing* the relationship. Think about it like this: Any relationship is the culmination of all the decisions each person has made to continue that relationship. Questions to consider:

1. What decisions did you make from the very beginning of your last relationship that solidified the status of the man from stranger to boyfriend? Think back to the beginning of how you met, the things you did together, and the first time you saw warning signs that made you a little nervous about your partner.

2. In general, how do you make your decisions? Do you tend to think things through and take time to act on them, or do you sometimes make quick, impulsive decisions?

3. What do the bad decisions you have made say about your personality style? Are you too trusting, naive, or dependent, or something else?

_____

THE TAKEAWAY

Many different factors make up your personality, but whether you are more introverted or extroverted is perhaps the most fundamental factor. The truth—as opposed to the myth—about this issue is that introversion and extroversion actually relates to how you recharge your emotional batteries. These questionnaires allowed you to consider this trait, as well as others, to give you a bird's-eye view of your personality and what fulfills you. The chapter's other exercises examined your core beliefs about yourself and your overall decision-making style. At this point, we are ready to move on to the next step of the insight stage. In that step, we will focus on the specifics of your relationships, including how you functioned in them and who you sought out as partners.

SELF-EVALUATION
Learning about Yourself

1. Looking back at all of your responses on the questionnaires, as well as your responses to the preceding exercises, would you say that you are more of an introvert or extrovert?

2. Which of the exercises or items on the questionnaire most surprised you? Why?

3. Which of the Helpless Core Beliefs best fit you? Which of the Unlovable Core Beliefs?

4. In terms of how you make decisions, how careful are you when it comes to deciding whom to date and whom to form a lasting relationship with?

5. Why do you think we examined your personality traits before getting into your past relationships?

CHAPTER 11

Your Relationship Story
Can You Detect the Patterns?

ENGAGING IN INSIGHT WORK can be interesting and fun, but it can also provoke a wide range of thoughts and feelings. In particular, recalling past painful experiences can elicit feelings of discomfort, anxiety, anger, and sadness. As you go through this process, trust that confronting the past has an important purpose. In my experience, this kind of in-depth examination is critical to help you break negative patterns and will help you to navigate your romantic future with greater awareness and caution.

The problem of repeating destructive relationship patterns is complex—it's not something that can be understood or resolved in an instant. Here, we'll look at how you function in relationships and at who you've chosen as partners, with the first part focused on you and the second part focused on your partners.

In the first part, you will examine how you approach and begin relationships, consider how you feel when your relationships end, determine your relationship strengths and weaknesses, and finally take inventory of your fundamental beliefs about romantic relationships. In the second part, you will consider your past partners and search for the common threads among them.

You in Your Past Relationships: Love's Beginning

In the next exercise, you will answer questions about your frame of mind at the time that you began your past relationships. As you engage in the exercise, make an effort to recall what your life was like at that point—where you lived, who you socialized with, and how you felt about yourself and your life then. Ask yourself whether a given period reflected you at your best, or perhaps you in a more vulnerable state.

EXERCISE: Approach to Relationships—The Beginning

1. At the beginning of my relationships, I usually feel:

   _____

2. At the beginning of my relationships, in terms of the future of the relationship, I am usually thinking that:

   _____

3. The trait that I look for the most at the beginning of my relationships is:

   _____

4. The traits that I watch out for—the warning signs in a man or a relationship—are:

   _____

5. When I am single, the reason that I want to find a relationship is:

   _____

6. If someone were to say to me that I jump too quickly into relationships, I would say:

_____

7. If someone were to say that I am too cautious in starting a relationship, I would say:

_____

8. In terms of sexual intercourse at the beginning of a relationship, I think it is important to wait the following length of time:

_____

9. Complaining frequently about my relationship is a sign that:

_____

10. I know my relationship is in trouble when I find myself:

_____

11. One of the lessons my past relationships have taught me is that I:

_____

I'm sure you know that there are no correct answers. The point of the exercise is to encourage you to consider your motivations, thoughts, and feelings at the time that you began your past relationships.

You in Your Past Relationships: Love's Ending

Let's move on to the next exercise, which will ask you to do something a little different but with the same goal—gaining insight into yourself and your past relationships. This involves a simple scale that asks you to think about how you felt when you ended past romantic relationships.

EXERCISE: When It's Over

Circle the number or word that applies to you, according to this scale:

Totally								*Not at all*
1	2	3	4	5	6	7	8	9

1. When my relationships end, I feel hopeless.

1	2	3	4	5	6	7	8	9

2. When my relationships end, I feel like I failed.

1	2	3	4	5	6	7	8	9

3. When my relationships end, I feel tired and emotionally spent.

1	2	3	4	5	6	7	8	9

4. When my relationships end, I feel as if my partner didn't truly understand or appreciate the essence of who I am.

1	2	3	4	5	6	7	8	9

5. When my relationships end, I feel embarrassed to tell others that another of my relationships did not last.

1	2	3	4	5	6	7	8	9

6. When my relationships end, I feel jealous of others who seem to have relationships without any problems.

1	2	3	4	5	6	7	8	9

7. When my relationships end, I feel angry at my last partner because he didn't turn out to be "The One."

   1   2   3   4   5   6   7   8   9

8. When my relationships end, I feel relieved that my partner is gone because I was unhappy in the relationship.

   1   2   3   4   5   6   7   8   9

9. When my relationships end, I feel eager to find someone else to take my old partner's place.

   1   2   3   4   5   6   7   8   9

Looking at Your Responses

Now that you have completed this quick task, take a look at the responses. Did some or all fall somewhere in the middle? Did some or all responses fall at one or both ends of the spectrum?

These questions should have prompted you to think about the feelings you have at the end of a relationship. I recall hearing a catchphrase in graduate school that explains the four simple categories of feelings, suggesting that most emotions fall into one of four: mad, sad, glad, and afraid.

Questions to Consider

1. Looking at your responses from the previous exercise, think about the four categories of feelings. If you had to choose one, which best describes your feelings when you end a relationship: mad, sad, glad, or afraid?

   _____

2. How aware were you of the feelings you had at the time, and to what extent did you try to block your feelings out?

_____

3. Perspective tends to change with time. How did time change what you thought about the quality of that relationship? A few months or even years later, how did you feel about your old relationships?

_____

Relationship Strengths and Weaknesses: Seven Key Ingredients

There are seven necessary ingredients to create and sustain a healthy, lasting relationship. If a given ingredient represents something you're good at, this factor is your relationship strength; if not, it's your relationship weakness. One way to determine your relationship strengths and weaknesses is to think about the feedback that partners have given you over the years. For example, in an argument, a partner might say, "I hate when you . . ." or "You always . . ." and then point out something that he takes issue with. You have probably also gotten some positive feedback over the years about things you do that are special or unique. You may have heard "I love it when you . . ." or "I'm glad that you . . ." when you said or did a certain type of thing. Here are some factors to consider when you take inventory of your relationship strengths and weaknesses.

1. Communication
2. Expressing yourself

3. Conflict resolution
4. Mood spectrum
5. Taking responsibility for your actions
6. Giving affection
7. Managing vulnerability/asking for help

Communication

In my experience counseling couples, "communication" is probably the word that comes up in sessions most frequently—it's a large umbrella under which many thoughts and feelings fall in a relationship. Communication is like a map you take on a road trip: If you have it, you can get to where you are going smoothly, even if the terrain is rocky, but without it, you can get lost.

One of the dynamics that I find many couples fall into over time is a passive-aggressive style of communication. This style of communication is just one of many communication styles, but it tends to be particularly destructive to a relationship. When taking inventory of your ability to communicate, think about the times that you have been most frustrated or upset in your current or last relationship. Consider these questions:

1. Overall, did you communicate in your past relationships clearly and directly from the beginning of the relationship until the end?

_____

2. Would your past partners partner say that you were a good or bad communicator? A direct communicator or a passive-aggressive communicator?

_____

3. If asked what behaviors you engaged in when you were very upset, what would your past partners say?

_____

_____

Expressing Yourself

When you are out of touch with your feelings, needs, and motivations, you have more of a tendency to repeat toxic patterns. Disconnectedness from your feelings and difficulty expressing yourself go hand in hand. As you take inventory of your relationship strengths and weaknesses, consider the wide range of feelings that a relationship can kick up—sadness, vulnerability, anger, and even rage—and examine how well you expressed the feelings. Consider these questions:

1. When you felt positive feelings toward your past partners, how did you typically express your fondness and appreciation? How often did you thank your partners for big and small gestures?

_____

_____

2. When you felt negative feelings toward your past partners, did you always express them? If so, how?

_____

_____

3. In general, did you tend to bottle up your feelings, or express them freely and directly?

_____

_____

Conflict Resolution

No matter how wonderful a relationship is, conflicts inevitably arise. Conflict and a small degree of arguing is actually a healthy sign in a relationship. Conflict shows that both people are mentally engaged in the relationship and have maintained their individual personalities. Problems arise, of course, if there is too much arguing or if a power struggle ensues between the partners. When it comes to conflict, the way you handle it reveals a great deal about you. Consider these questions:

1. When conflicts arose in past relationships, did you tend to overreact or react impulsively, or did you wait to hear all the details before deciding how to feel or what to do in response?

   _____

2. When you argued, were you able to do so in a way that maintained respect for yourself and for your partner?

   _____

3. In terms of your specific behaviors—what you said and did—how were you able to express your frustration or anger while simultaneously letting your partner know that you still loved and respected him?

   _____

4. During a conflict, did you usually see your partner as a member of the same team as you, or did it turn into a power struggle in which your partner seemed more like an opponent?

   _____

Mood Spectrum

No two human beings have exactly the same life history or bio-chemical makeup—each person is unique. Accordingly, we all fall in different places on the mood spectrum. On one end are people who are incredibly consistent, rarely appearing sad, angry, or even very happy—they simply appear even-keeled. On the other end of the spectrum are people whose moods run all over the map: One day they are happy, the next day they are angry; one moment they are depressed, the next moment they're elated. Most people fall somewhere in the middle. Understanding your mood is critical to understanding your personality, your behavior, and the effect you have on others. What's more, understanding your mood and its impact is critical to relationships because your mood is like the gas that fuels the car—it is, in large part, the basis for your thoughts, feelings, and behavior. Consider these questions:

1. What feedback have your past partners given you about your moods?

_____

2. Overall, how would you describe how your mood was in your past relationships?

_____

3. What impact did your mood have on your past relationships? How consistent was your mood in those relationships?

_____

4. If you lived with a past partners, how did living with someone affect your daily mood? Was it easy or difficult to live with a partner?

_____

Taking Responsibility for Your Actions

We all have faults. No surprise there: Because we are not machines or computers, we are all prone to real-life flaws and eccentricities. Life can be difficult and unpredictable, and temporary and permanent stressors don't make it any easier for us. When things go wrong, people are likely to attribute their misfortune to all sorts of different causes. While some people are willing to own some responsibility, others may shift the responsibility or blame to someone else. To determine whether taking responsibility is a relationship strength or weakness for you, try to recall a time when you had a major disagreement with a past partner, and then consider these questions:

1. How did you validate your partner's feelings during a major argument? In other words, how did you (or did you at all) acknowledge that your partner had a right to feel that way?

_____

2. What concessions did you make during the argument regarding what you could have done differently to avoid an escalation of that problem?

_____

3. When you knew that you were at fault for something, how did you communicate this to your partner?

_____

4. Sometimes during an argument, it appears that one person needs to have the last word. How did this apply to you in past relationships?

_____

5. How often in your relationships did you reflect on what your partner said during an argument and later apologize after further reflection?

_____

6. Which of your personality traits made it difficult for you to take responsibility for your part in the creation of a relationship problem? Which traits made it easy?

_____

Giving Affection

Giving physical affection is an important component of a healthy relationship. How affectionate you are indicates how comfortable you are showing emotion and how you feel about your partner in general. When it comes to affection, how you give it and how you feel about your partner are complex factors. For instance, you could be someone who loves showing affection but who has built up so much resentment toward your partner that you have no interest in showing signs of love and affection. On the other hand, you could be someone who truly loves and feels good about your partner but who feels uncomfortable or awkward expressing love and affection. The important message here is this: Showing affection—holding hands, rubbing your partner's back, and offering your partner a kiss for the heck of it—is a cornerstone of any good relationship. Affection reminds us that we are loved and that we are safe, and how easily you give it indicates whether this is a relationship strength or weakness for you. Consider these questions:

1. How frequently did you touch your partner in past relationships? Try to recall the ways that you extended a loving touch—one that was not intended to lead to sex.

_____

2. How frequently did you kiss your partner on the cheek, the lips, on the hand? Every day? Once per week? Once per month?

_____

3. How comfortable were you in terms of giving physical affection to your partner in front of others? Think about the following behaviors: holding hands, kissing on the lips, putting your arm around your partner or letting your partner put his arm around you?

_____

4. What feedback have you received from past partners about how much you expressed your love and appreciation by giving them physical affection?

_____

Managing Vulnerability/Asking for Help

A good relationship—romantic or otherwise—requires intimacy between two people. Until I received years of clinical training and began to specialize in relationship issues, my conception of intimacy was a little misguided. I—probably like many others—believed that intimacy referred to a sexual or romantic feeling you have for someone. Over time, however, I learned that the true meaning of intimacy refers to trust and honesty in a relationship. Contrary to my initial understanding, intimacy actually involves the process through which two people can feel loved, honestly show who they are, and work through difficulties together. Intimacy requires that you let your guard down and trust that your partner will not take advantage of you. Intimacy also requires that you trust your partner to not hurt you intentionally. To create and sustain intimacy in a relationship, each person must feel comfortable expressing his or her vulnerability and must accordingly feel open to asking for physical and emotional help when needed.

As you go through difficult experiences in life, it helps to be able to ask for help from your partner—to seek out a shoulder to lean on when you are anxious, afraid, or uncomfortable. As important as vulnerability is to intimacy, and as important as intimacy is to a good relationship, vulnerability can be incredibly difficult for some people to feel, and even more to painful to show to others. Consider the following questions and think about how comfortable you are feeling vulnerable. In particular, think about how your management of vulnerable feelings may have impacted your past relationships.

1. Quick word association: What is the first thing that comes to mind when you think of the word "vulnerability?" Are your associations positive or negative?

_____

2. How comfortable are you telling your partner you need some extra love or attention when you are feeling down or overwhelmed?

_____

3. How comfortable are you feeling vulnerable and asking for help with your friends and family? Should there be a difference between how you feel in this area with your partner as opposed to others close to you?

_____

Relationship Beliefs

While the previous exercise asked you to focus on your past partners and relationships, the next exercise will focus on your beliefs about relationships in general. In this exercise, you will not be asked to remember a certain partner or think about a specific past relationship. Instead, you will simply take a step back and look at what your overall expectations are in terms of romantic relationships.

EXERCISE: Your Relationship Beliefs

Answer the following questions to take inventory of your most basic relationship beliefs.

1. What are three of the most important characteristics to look for in a partner?

    _____

2. What is the primary purpose of a romantic relationship?

    _____

3. What is the main difference between a good relationship and a bad relationship?

    _____

4. How do you know when it is time to end a relationship?

    _____

5. Should relationships be hard or easy?

   _____

6. To what degree can a boyfriend change who he is?

   _____

7. What are examples of behaviors or traits that a boyfriend can change during the course of a relationship? What are examples of behaviors or traits that probably won't change?

   _____

8. In a good relationship, how much time should two people spend together?

   _____

9. How much time should two people in a relationship spend with other friends (socializing without each other)?

   _____

10. How do you feel about two people in a relationship having same-sex and opposite-sex friends? What do you do if you think it's okay but a new boyfriend thinks it's not?

   _____

11. Is arguing good or bad in a relationship?

_____

12. If you and a partner have an argument, is raising your voice okay? Is yelling ever okay? If so, in what circumstances would yelling be okay?

_____

13. What is the best way to resolve problems in a relationship?

_____

14. How important is sex to a long-term relationship?

_____

15. How sexually attracted should a person feel toward a prospective partner at the beginning of a relationship?

_____

16. If someone told you that you should like a boyfriend as much as you like your best friend, what would you say in response?

_____

Your Partners in Past Relationships

We are going to move now from your relationship beliefs to your past romantic partners. In the next exercise, you will be asked to take an overall picture of who your past partners were and to answer the questions accordingly. Remember, don't get caught in the details or focus too much on one particular past boyfriend. The exercise is designed to help you detect the patterns at work that had a role in determining who you chose as past partners. Keep in mind that the exercise below is only a primer. The final section of my program will focus on skills and exercises you can use to kiss potential exes goodbye forever!

EXERCISE: Common Threads Among Past Partners

1. Though my past partners were all different in obvious ways, a few personality traits they all shared include:

   _____

2. In general, my past partners treated me:

   _____

3. Some behaviors that most or all of my past partners engaged in that made me feel upset or anxious include:

   _____

4. When it came to talking about my day, needing help, or talking about my feelings, I usually felt like my partners:

   _____

5. My past partners showed me that they loved me by:

_____

6. In terms of how financially stable my past partners were, I would say most or all of them were:

_____

7. In terms of how emotionally stable my past partners were, I would say most or all of them were:

_____

8. When it comes to the true character of my past partners—how caring, honest, and consistent they were—I would say they:

_____

9. The trait of my past partners that bothered me the most was:

_____

10. The trait of my past partners that I liked the most was:

_____

11. Overall, the main feeling my past partners elicited in me was:

_____

Now that you've taken the time to deeply examine your history, look closely at your responses. They not only tell you about who your past partners were but also about who *you* were when you were in a relationship with them. After all, no one forces us to start a relationship, right? Relationships are voluntary. There's an expression that says you should look to see who someone's friends are to figure out who that person is. The expression wisely acknowledges that who we choose as friends speaks volumes about what we are drawn to, what we expect from relationships, and how we believe we are supposed to be treated.

THE TAKEAWAY

Taking inventory of your past relationships and partners, as well as your beliefs about relationships in general, is a huge step toward changing your approach. Conventional wisdom tells us that we must learn from history to avoid repeating mistakes, and navigating relationships is no exception to this rule. The ability to detect the common thread among past partners, in conjunction with awareness of how you feel when a relationship ends and what you believe about relationships in general, is critical to changing your ways and breaking your cycle of repetition. In the next chapter, with this new insight, you can delve into what I call your life circumstances story and gain a more full perspective of how you operate overall—as an individual and as one-half of a couple.

SELF-EVALUATION
Maturing Through Reflection

1. Which traits did your partners most commonly share?

2. Why do you think you sought out partners with those traits?

3. In comparison to how you felt when your past relationships ended, how would you like to feel if a future relationship were to end?

4. What is the healthiest message you can give yourself when a relationship ends?

CHAPTER 12

Your Life Circumstances Story

What Needs to Change?

RELATIONSHIP BOOKS OBVIOUSLY FOCUS on the relationships themselves and the people within those relationships. However, I believe that such a restricted focus is part of the problem. It's easy to focus on the men and the past relationships. Right now, it is time to pay more attention not just to your personality (as you did in Chapter 10) and not just on your past relationships (as you did in Chapter 11) but to the many nonromantic areas of your life that, I believe, have a major impact on your choice of partners and how long you stay in an unhappy relationship.

As such, it's time to go through a series of inventories that deal with less obvious "life" factors that can help round out the comprehensive picture of why you suffer from RRS. Again, you are devoting time and energy to these thorough inventories because insight helps prompt real change.

Your Overall Life Satisfaction

Since RRs tend to restrict themselves to a narrow selection of potential partners—usually seeking out the same toxic type of partner again and again—other parts of their lives may be restricted as well. In other words, RRs often lack true balance in their lives.

One necessary component to breaking the repetition cycle is to learn how to have greater perspective and balance in your life. Although a bad relationship or toxic partner is the elephant hogging the room, stop and think about how this elephant could be distracting you from examination of other key areas in your life. These other areas must function well in order for you to find and maintain a loving, lasting relationship.

Think about the connection between your relationship and the other parts of your life in the following way:

How you feel about your life *overall* influences HOW you feel about your relationship. How you feel about your life *overall* influences WHOM you seek out for relationships.

Your Career

Since you probably spend more time at work than you do most other places, it makes sense to take inventory of how fulfilled you feel by your career. Think about your career in broad terms. For some of you, your career is a full- or part-time job; for others, it might be pursuing an educational degree or working at home as a stay-at-home mom. Regardless of what your career is, how you feel about your work has a *lot* to do with how happy or unhappy you feel in general.

EXERCISE: Career Satisfaction

To get a good gauge of your career satisfaction, answer the questions as honestly as possible.

1. On a scale of 1 to 10 (10 being the highest), how fulfilling is your career?

2. What do you like about your job? What do you dislike about your job?

_____

3. What is a career goal that you believe is possible to achieve?

_____

4. What have you done in the past three months to achieve this goal?

_____

5. How close are you to achieving your career goal?

_____

Your Friendships

Many RRs have sat in my office and said with certainty, "My friendships are great, but my relationships with men are the problem." When learning to heal your romantic relationships, you must take inventory of all your relationships, romantic and otherwise. Sometimes, when I'm working with clients, we begin to discover that things aren't so rosy in any of their friendships. In this next exercise, you will take inventory of your friendships and ideally will gain insight into the pivotal role friendships play in your overall degree of life fulfillment.

EXERCISE: Friendships

To understand how your friendships affect your life, answer the questions as honestly as possible.

1. On a scale of 1 to 10, how fulfilling are your friendships and social life?

   _____

2. What is one thing missing in your friendships or social life?

   _____

3. What have you done in the past three months to create a more fulfilling social life?

   _____

4. Do you feel that you have a sufficient number of close friends?

   _____

5. To what extent do you have friends to whom you can turn for emotional support and to express your true feelings when you are upset?

   _____

6. Do you have friends who make you laugh?

   _____

7. Do you have different types of friends to complement the various sides of your personality and interests?

_____

8. When you are in a relationship, to what extent do you socialize with friends without your partner present?

_____

Interests and Hobbies

It's time to turn your attention to the hobbies and interests in your life—the activities that nourish you and renew your energy and spirit. Again, how fulfilled you feel in your life—and, indirectly, in your relationships—is intimately related to how fulfilled you feel in this area of your life.

EXERCISE: Interests and Hobbies

To understand the role that hobbies play in your life, answer the questions as honestly as possible.

1. My three favorite hobbies are:

_____

2. The hobby or interest that I invest the most time in is:

_____

3. If someone asked if I have enough hobbies, I would say:

_____

4. Hobbies are important for my mental health because:

_____

5. Investing time in regular hobbies is good for my romantic relationships because:

_____

6. If I don't currently have enough hobbies or engage in a hobby regularly, one reason I might consider pursuing one would be:

_____

Personal Health

One of the most important areas of your life is your personal health, which encompasses both your physical health and your mental health. Take a look at the inventories that follow and answer the brief questions.

EXERCISE: Physical and Mental Health

1. How do you feel about your current weight? Is it something you feel okay with or something that you want to change?

_____

2. If you believe your weight needs to change, what is your goal weight?

_____

3. If you believe your weight needs to change, what are you currently doing to reach your weight goal?

_____

4. What is your current weekly exercise routine? Do you have any specific exercise goals?

_____

5. Are there any behaviors that you engage in that are bad for your health? If so, what plans have you made to stop engaging in this behavior?

_____

6. How would you describe your current energy level? Answer this question based on your usual energy level from day to day.

_____

7. How would you describe your usual mood from day to day?

_____

8. If you feel anxious or depressed on a fairly regular basis, have you consulted a doctor or a mental health therapist?

_____

Charity

I believe that happy people make good and happy partners, and some of the happiest people I know are some of the most charitable and generous. I often think of an expression I once heard: The best way to feel better about yourself is to do something for somebody else. By extension, charity is good for your relationships, too, because how you feel about yourself goes a long way toward impacting the health of the relationship.

There are countless ways to give. You may recently have heard about high-profile examples of charitable giving—billionaires including Warren Buffett and Bill Gates have donated billions of dollars to charity. However, you don't need to be a billionaire to give, because you can give in so many different ways. For example, I have a friend who spends a couple of hours serving warm food on Thanksgiving at a homeless shelter. While his giving may appear different from that of a person who writes a check for a political donation or a nonprofit service project, it all falls under the same umbrella: Giving acknowledges the larger world you live in and demonstrates that through action, you're determined to make it better.

Take some time to reflect on the following questions regarding charity.

EXERCISE: Charity

1. The last time I gave my time or money to a charitable organization was:

   _____

2. When I give my time or money, I later feel:

   _____

3. If I had to choose a type of organization I would most like to volunteer for (animal rescue, poverty eradication, child mentoring, etc.), I would choose:

   _____

4. If I were asked how many hours per month I would be willing to engage in some type of volunteer work, I would say:

   _____

5. If I have not spent much time giving to charitable organizations in the past year, it is because:

   _____

THE TAKEAWAY

Repeating toxic relationship patterns is easy to do without awareness of your motivations and behavior. In taking the preceding life circumstances inventories, you may have gleaned this chapter's ultimate point: You will be less prone to repeat toxic patterns and seek out or stay in bad relationships if the other areas in your life are fulfilling you. Conversely, if any of these areas are out of whack, you will be more likely to go down a rocky relationship road. That's because, as an old clinical mentor of mine used to say, **everything is related.** You must take inventory of your level of fulfillment with your career, social life, and other areas in order to see if any of those need fixing along with your romantic life. This isn't meant to overwhelm but to motivate you! The reason for doing all of this work is that in the end, if you're happier and more fulfilled in life, you'll be a happier and more fulfilled romantic partner.

SELF-EVALUATION
How Well-Rounded Are You?

1. When you took inventory of your satisfaction with your career, what did you determine?

2. When you took inventory of your social life, what (if anything) did you determine is missing?

3. If you could add one type of person to your social life—dream boyfriend excluded—describe who the person would be and what characteristics that person would have.

4. Why are hobbies important for your overall life satisfaction?

5. How can investing in charity be good for your relationships?

PART IV

Behaviors New to You— Reshaping Your Approach to Relationships

CHAPTER 13

Mourning the Loss

Sounds Easier Than It Is

AFTER A GREAT DEAL of work and emotional energy spent, you have
reached the part that focuses on the behaviors that lead to recovery.
Together, we'll walk through the steps required to break your repetition cycle. If we were healing a broken leg instead of a broken approach
to relationships, this would be the point at which we apply the cast.
And just like a doctor would tell you to stay off your leg for a while or
keep it elevated, there are specific instructions I'm going to ask you to
follow to eradicate RRS. Given some time and a concerted effort to
adhere to the prescription, you'll develop a new, empowered attitude
toward forming relationships.

The first important step in this recovery process is mourning the
loss of your former relationship identity and the years of pain that
came with repeating with the wrong partners. This mourning process is critical because it involves getting in touch with your feelings.
Because RRs often act out their feelings rather than reflecting on
them, confrontation of these often-avoided feelings is an easily over-
looked—but crucial—step toward change. In fact, if I had to isolate
the single most important step in creating change and moving on from
a painful past, I would choose mourning the loss. Mourning the loss

is an essential stage of any grieving process—and you, my friend, have some grieving to do.

So what is it exactly that you need to grieve? First, let me explain that when you mourn a loss, you grieve for the fact that you must part with something to which you are attached. That which is lost can be tangible (like a family heirloom with sentimental value); it can be event-related (perhaps you didn't get a promotion that you hoped for); or it can be emotional (think of the sudden loss of trust that occurs when someone betrays you).

When it comes to you and your tendency to repeat a dysfunctional relationship pattern, you must mourn the loss in three different ways: You must mourn for what happened in the past, for the losses that still pain you today, and for the uncertainty of what the future will bring. We will now look more closely at each of these processes and examine how, in your case, you need to proceed in your mourning process.

Mourning the Loss: Past

The most obvious loss you face comes in the form of a romantic relationship—or, more likely, several of them. Look back at your relationships, and consider the amount of time and energy you spent feeling all kinds of unpleasant feelings—anxiety, anger, sadness, confusion, emptiness, and frustration.

Reflecting on these past failed relationships, imagine that you're watching a friend going through these experiences. It would be difficult to end a tearful phone call with her knowing that she's going to bed with a pit in her stomach, or to look across at her at a girls' night dinner and see a flat, gray face where you used to see a laughing one. In short, it would pain you to see your friend in pain. Once you conjure these images in your mind, remember that the woman you're imagining is actually you. Let yourself feel the same compassion for your own pain that you would for a close friend's.

As you begin to mourn the loss, you will move through, and then past, the sadness if you let yourself recall specific past circumstances. Try to remember a specific day when you hit your relationship's rock bottom and felt like you had almost nothing left inside you. When you recall that day, let yourself feel sympathy for what you went through.

As you mourn the loss for what happened in the past, ask yourself whether things had to turn out this way. The truth is that you weren't programmed to be unhappy or miserable, so go ahead and let yourself feel upset when you think about why your journey has been so difficult when it comes to love. You can probably pull up the names of a few happy couples, people who seem to make love look so easy. There's no satisfying answer for why some women have been dealt less pain in their love lives than you have. It's clearly not fair that your journey has been filled with repeating, while others' journeys may seem peaceful and happy. Again, the reasons why you have had to suffer—regardless of whatever set the stage for that suffering—aren't fair. Yet lingering on a sense of injustice will get you nowhere fast, so for now, just let yourself lament what you've had to go through.

There's no reason to continue suffering and hovering on the out-skirts of real love—it's time to go after the real thing. In order to stop repeating relationship patterns and start falling for men who are good for you, you must mourn the fact that love, for you, has not turned out so well. Understand that I'm not encouraging you to throw yourself a giant self-pity party and crown yourself a victim, but rather encouraging you to tell it like it is so that you can later move on. Only when you accept reality will you be able to live in reality successfully.

Mourning the Loss: Present Losses

As you filled out the Insight Inventories, I asked you some pretty serious open-ended questions. Among those, I asked you what the purpose of a relationship is. My answer to this question is simple: to grow.

For most women, growth can occur literally, by growing a family; or figuratively, by evolving and maturing and using the relationship as a springboard to live a fulfilling and dynamic life in and outside of the home.

The great tragedy of relationship repeating is that unfulfilling relationships cause you to regress rather than to move forward. Now that you've decided to stop repeating, you have the opportunity to look at your life and figure out where to go from here. What could you have been doing with all the time you spent stuck in a repetitious rut? Think about your career, skills you could have been honing, the family you may have dreamed of, and your other goals. When you repeat toxic relationship patterns, you merely survive your relationships—you don't move forward or grow.

Without fail, my clients successfully recovering from the repetition cycle all of a sudden find themselves investing in parts of their lives that they long ago tucked away. Once they are free of the albatross of repetition, I see these clients suddenly focusing more on their career and a promotion at work, or joining a social group and cultivating a hobby. Having retired from a career of relationship drama, they suddenly find themselves with time and mental energy to devote to things *other* than their relationship—just *imagine!*

As you mourn the loss of your present circumstances, grieve for the holes in your life today that have gone unnoticed because of your relationship distractions. If you have fitness goals, let yourself feel sympathy for your body, which you may not have not cared for in the way it deserves—smoking due to anxiety, overeating due to sadness or festering resentments, and so on. If you have taken focus away from your work, acknowledge that it's time to pay attention again to your career goals. It never fails: when you're in a good relationship, the rest of your life flourishes, but when you're in a bad relationship, other areas of your life have a tendency to wilt away, thanks to inadequate care and attention.

Mourning the Loss: Future Losses

As a mental health professional, I can guarantee you that hard work and an honest effort to change is often rewarded with happier life circumstances. At the same time, I know that you don't yet have any proof that change is possible. I also know that it's a lot to ask of you to have faith and hope when things haven't gone so well in the past. In fact, some of your fears and anxieties are probably well founded. The future can be scary. This lack of a clear path and a clear outcome ahead of you is something we can briefly bemoan together.

I wish that you didn't have to make any changes at all, that your terrific partner could be watching television in the next room, getting ready to make dinner for you and your family. Having such a foundation would certainly make the future a little less daunting. Because I am asking you to try to change and to abandon your old relationship ways, I know that you will confront the unknown. That you must plunge into the future without a romantic partner by your side is a loss. Though I know that you will grow from this experience and emerge stronger as a result, I also have sympathy for the fact that making the switch to a new relationship identity can be one of the toughest parts of the journey.

In this chapter, we'll go through several more exercises that will help you to mourn your losses, and mark a critical step in burying your old identity. To begin this journey, you'll need to purchase a new notebook or find one lying around the house. You should name this notebook and indicate that name on its cover. I recommend that you call it your Changes Journal, as this is what your new journal will be documenting.

In filling out the Identity Inventories, you have already recorded important information that relates to your personality style, past partners, and overall life circumstances. In your new journal, I want you to jot down any thoughts or feelings that pop up as you begin to form your new-and-improved identity. There is a method to my madness: There are few techniques that I find as effective as writing in creating change. When you write, you archive your thoughts, organize and solidify them, and see them on paper. I am confident that you'll find journaling to be an important—no, *necessary*—outlet as you engage in the following exercises focusing on mourning the loss.

Opening the Floodgates

Once you begin to look at your dysfunctional relationship patterns under the microscope, you may soon find yourself reviewing your every thought, move, and motivation as they apply to men and your relationships with them. It's somewhat similar to the experience psychology graduate school students go through as they first learn about a potpourri of serious mental disorders—the students fear they meet the criteria for nearly every diagnosis! Becoming aware of problems can have a disorienting effect, causing you to question yourself and to rethink things that were once set in stone. In fact, the process of change can introduce a host of uncertainties—and this onslaught is actually a good thing. I always tell my clients that the goal is to confront and examine (not to mention *feel*) all of your feelings so that you can effectively do what you wanted to do in the first place: move past them.

I recently watched an episode of *The Oprah Winfrey Show* in which the popular singer-songwriter Carly Simon openly discussed her lifelong battle with depression. She described how she copes with the depression when it comes: She gives in to it completely, rather than fight it or try to wish it away. The singer explained that indulging the depression in its entirety actually helps her eventually move past it, rather than half-experience it for a longer period of time. In a similar vein, I encourage you to indulge all of your feelings when it comes to mourning the loss.

When I hear my clients talk about their chosen coping mechanisms for handling a breakup, I often gather that they're attempting to cut out certain emotions by fabricating more pleasant ones. One particular client, for instance, only listens to fast, upbeat music and swears off any sad music that will remind her of how upset she feels underneath it all. But often, the thing you least want to do is the very thing you need to do the most.

Music

I suggest that you take a period of a week or so and listen to all the sad music you can. Now, don't drive yourself into a suicidal stupor, but it is important that you stimulate the feelings of sadness that surely lie deeply buried—or not so deeply buried—inside you after years of repeating relationships that went nowhere. If you need to set the mood, don't hesitate to light some candles, turn off your phones, and play some melancholic music. Again, the point is to confront the sadness and let it wash over you, so that you can then move beyond it.

Movies

Music isn't the only vehicle that can help you to access your inner sadness, anger, or disappointment. Movies can help unearth all kinds of feelings—happiness, hopefulness, and, of course, some of the darker feelings, as well. It's a true testament to the power of your unconscious mind that you can sometimes find yourself watching a film that elicits feelings you didn't even know you had. For instance, have you ever been watching a movie and found that you cried a little harder than you would have expected? When this happens, the film is tapping directly into feelings of sadness and loss that you managed to push down into the remotest corners of your awareness—you know the ones, with creaky floorboards and spider webs thick enough to catch a fly ball.

Too often in my practice, I see clients who try to bury or deny altogether their feelings after a breakup. No one likes admitting feelings of desperation and loss, so avoidance is understandable to some degree. The unfortunate reality is that it is precisely those suffering from a failed relationship who need to confront and express their feelings most. For these clients, my prescription involves tearjerkers. To help you mourn the loss of your old identity—that of a woman who has felt unfulfilled in relationship after relationship—I recommend that you take a trip to the video store and give yourself a weekend to watch a few sad movies, particularly those that focus on relationships.

Although everyone is entitled to mourn in her own unique way, my work with clients over the years has shown me that one of the most effective ways to grieve is to cry, and a tearjerker almost certainly accesses sad feelings and allows you to purge them. If you don't consciously feel sad, these films will remind you of what likely lurks just beneath the surface after years of accumulating romantic wounds.

The Baby Photo

As you mourn the loss of your old relationship identity, you are going to need a baby photo of yourself. Search around the house or call one of your relatives—parent, grandparent, aunt, or uncle—and ask that he or she send you one.

With your baby photo in hand, you are going to talk to the baby as if that little baby were someone else. Though you may think this is silly or can't figure out how it relates, I need you to take a leap of faith and trust the process. I swear by this exercise after having watched its impact on many clients! Talk to the baby using your knowledge of what her future with men would entail. Look at that innocent child in the photo and think about how many romantic heartbreaks she would suffer at the hands of men who weren't good for her. Now, I want you to apologize to that baby for all the pain she'll suffer as a result of your romances, and explain that you did the best you could to protect her from any suffering. As you talk to her, you are going to explain that you are giving up your old relationship identity and making room for a better one that's on its way. In the following, you can trace the experience of my client Megan as she conducted this exercise and later told me about it in our session. She didn't have a lot to say, but the few words she did say spoke volumes.

> *Megan,*
> *You look so pure and innocent here, with your little green dress and your hair barely reaching your eyes. You were never supposed to feel like this—so unhappy, like a failure. You weren't programmed to be alone. You deserved to be happy and to find someone worth loving. From now on, you are going to see just how good things can be. I am going to do a better job of protecting you from now on because I want you to be as happy and hopeful as you look in this picture.*

Conventional wisdom suggests that therapists are neutral, objective guides, but the truth was that Megan's one-on-one with her baby photo broke my heart. Her candor and honesty reminded me of why I do the work that I do—why I love helping people to heal. She was right: No one deserves to feel lost or hopeless. It is the right of each of us as human beings to have the potential of hope ahead of us. Sadly, Megan began to realize as she worked through the exercises that her repeating toxic patterns had weakened a place deep inside her—the place that generates hope and faith. You will see that in the next exercises you do, you'll continue mourning the loss of your old identity with the ultimate goal of creating one that firmly believes, "I can and will find a love that lasts."

Purging the Reminders

Among the exercises I want you to do to successfully mourn the loss of your old relationship identity is a fairly basic one—getting rid of painful reminders. Your immediate environment may be littered with reminders of a past partner, or there may be few or no reminders that you keep in plain sight. To complete this exercise, you are going to need to create a unique storage place—perhaps a small cardboard box or dresser drawer—where you will compartmentalize all physical reminders of your exes. If you prefer, you can name it something simple like The Ex Box or whatever name appeals to you. The point is that you are gathering the reminders in one place and putting them away.

Some of the reminders are obvious—framed pictures and the like—but other, less obvious items can remind you of a past partner as well. If your past partner gave you a puppy, please don't get rid of the dog, but let's put all inanimate reminders on notice! Take a thorough look around your home and determine whether there are any items that were given to you by past partners as gifts. If so, they go in your Ex Box. After you've inspected your living environment, check your car, your workspace, and any other areas where you spend time and tend to accumulate personal belongings.

Once you've done a surface inspection, you need to ask yourself where other items from past partners may be stored—letters, e-mails, or other gifts. The items could include clothing or jewelry, books, and so forth. Gather all items that are reminders of past exes—I don't care how long ago that relationship ended or how *over* a given ex-boyfriend you think you are—and put them away in a clearly marked box, drawer, or storage unit (depending on how many exes there have been!).

I don't need to review with you the reasons why purging the reminders of past partners is critical. If you really want to mourn the loss of the old you, who was drawn to and stuck around for all the partners with whom you were ultimately incompatible, you must start with a clean slate. With this exercise, and those to follow, your new behaviors are making a subtle announcement to yourself and to the world that things are changing.

The Written Word

I emphasize writing as much as I do because I have watched so many patients transform their lives for the better upon learning how to heal themselves through writing.

For years, research has confirmed what psychologists and avid journalers have long known to be true: Converting your worries, triumphs, and stories into written language can have remarkable curative effects. In their article "Forming a Story: The Health Benefits of Narrative," authors James Pennebaker and Janel Seagal review the research and summarize that, in asking college students to write about their personal experiences, "the writing exercise improved their physical health, resulted in better grades, and often changed their lives." They add that more recently, researchers have found that keeping a journal improves blood markers of immune functioning. Pennebaker and Seagal suggest that perhaps the reason why writing about our experiences is so helpful is because it allows us to construct a tidy, logical narrative of our lives and organize our emotions in a way that few other activities do. "By integrating thoughts and feelings," they write, "the person can then construct more easily a coherent narrative of the experience. Once formed, the event can now be summarized, stored, and forgotten more efficiently." Given these findings, you, too, can benefit from writing about your thoughts and feelings.

Letter to Your Exes

In this exercise, you are going to make a formal announcement, almost like a press release to be sent over the newswires: I am going to ask you to write a letter to your exes. Imagine that a group of your exes has gathered in a room and is lined up against a wall. To help you flesh out the visual picture, give the image some depth by making the wall they stand against your favorite color, and decide whether your exes will wear formal or casual clothing. You are going to write a letter to read to all of these men at once, and it will make the announcement that you are giving up your old relationship identity and will be deliberately constructing a new one as a result of your experiences with them.

As you read this, perhaps you are single and you sought out this book because it's going to help you forge better relationships in the future, but some of you may still be entwined in an unhealthy relationship. If you're in the latter group, you can still participate in this exercise—simply address your letter to your current partner and don't give it to him unless you decide *later* that giving it to him is what you really want to do.

As you prepare to write your letter, take a look back at the inventories you filled out in Chapter 11 about your past relationships. After a quick glance at your responses, I think you will find that this letter practically writes itself! Specifically, think about your partners and ask yourself what needs they met and what needs they did not meet.

After a relationship ends, or even while you're still in it, there are many thoughts and feelings that you wish—in retrospect—that you could have expressed. An unsent letter is the perfect way to say what you need to say, and a satisfying way to move away from the myth that you need closure with the actual man who caused you emotional pain in order to move on.

Let me take a moment here to explain why the supposedly soothing experience of getting closure—say, by e-mailing or shouting or even calmly asking the typical post-breakup ream of questions—is pure myth. I always tell my clients who struggle with repeating that the only way to actually get closure is to stop trying to get it.

Breaking news: The real person you need closure with is yourself.

In the end, you are the one who calls the shots; the one who makes the decision to keep repeating or to find someone different with whom you are emotionally compatible.

Here's a short letter written by my client Valerie when she participated in this exercise. She took the letter from her purse, somewhat crinkled after what I guessed to be many readings of it. What Valerie wrote will give you an example of one type of letter, but your letter will obviously reflect your own thoughts, feelings, and experiences as they relate to your situation. Remember, there's no reason to be anything but completely open and honest here.

Dear Exes,

I'm writing because I'm angry. I wasted so much time with you. I should have known from the start what a dead-end street it would be to try to have a relationship with you. I can never get those years back—they're lost.

I don't know what I was thinking, believing things would get better. If I met you today, I wouldn't waste a single minute with you. All you ever cared about was what you wanted. No one forced me to stay but you sure were good at manipulating me to stay. At least now I have the future. Trust me when I say I will be more careful next time, because there will never be another chance for men like you in my life. I'm done with the drama and altogether wash my hands of you.

Valerie

You can practically feel the anger and heat emanating from her letter. Valerie did a good job of tapping into a boiling vat of resentment that she clearly still carries. Now it's your turn; try writing your own.

The Burial Pilgrimage

Memory studies suggest that we best remember the things that come last in a series of activities or facts. For that reason, I saved the burial pilgrimage for the final mourning exercise because it's the most helpful one you can do.

Since the beginning of time, death has been connected with various burial rituals. So many rituals exist to honor the dead because a special behavior denoting the end of one's life helps to crystallize the fact that something important has been lost. In the same way, I want you to realize that something has been lost in your life—the "old you" that would permit the repetition of bad relationship patterns—and you need to signify this loss with a ritual.

Visit an Actual Cemetery

There are a few different ways to conduct the exercise. Among the possibilities, the most effective and powerful option is to take a trip to a local cemetery. While many people consider cemeteries to be creepy or disturbing spots, you can also see them as peaceful and beautiful, depending on the lens you use. Although I have never been one to visit cemeteries for a good time, I can appreciate what some others see in them—the solace, the sanctity, the peacefulness of souls whose bodies gave out but whose essences live on in the people who remember them. In the heart of Los Angeles, for example, lies a beautiful old cemetery, called Hollywood Forever, known originally as the resting place for Hollywood stars and now, as well, as the location for outdoor movie screenings in the summer. That a cemetery can be appreciated for being something far from creepy is reassuring, and can remind you, as you consider this next exercise, that cemeteries can serve many positive functions.

As you embark on your own burial pilgrimage, think about the bigger picture and let yourself stretch a bit to reap the optimal benefit from it. For those of you who take the trip to the cemetery and conduct your burial ritual there, let your mind wander. Think about death or the perishing of something once alive but now gone, and how death has impacted your life so far. At first, you may think about the people in your life who have passed away. But also let your mind wander to other things in your life—the intangible ones—that you have lost. What experiences caused you to lose your trust in strangers? In lovers? Those losses must be buried, too, in their own sorts of cemeteries.

Finally, look out over the sea of tombstones and actually imagine that a tombstone in the distance is the old you—the you who spent all that time repeating, loving and losing, and going for broke each time. Imagine that the tombstone is the brokenhearted you or the self-blaming you. Now, in this moment, talk to yourself or announce out loud that your old relationship identity is passing. Please keep in mind that there are no correct ways to do this exercise—only the ways that make sense for you. One of my patients, Candice, conducted her burial pilgrimage and recounted what the experience was like for her.

At first it felt kind of strange being there in the cemetery by myself. But then I just decided I would let it be kind of a quick, simple thing. I looked over to the next hill and I fixed my eyes on a tombstone that looked pretty nondescript. Imagining it with my own name on it felt a bit too morbid for me, so I just imagined that it said something like, "Here lies a lot of bad relationships, and the identity of the woman who actually put up with them." I tried to think of myself—the actual me, standing in the cemetery looking around—as lighter and cleaner after burying the old identity. I have to say, it felt good. My chest and shoulders lifted a little with the thought. And then I actually said out loud, "Rest in peace— and don't ever think about showing up in my life again." Then I walked back to my car and went home. As I drove away, I wondered what I'd think about when I passed by that cemetery from now on.

I, too, wondered what she'd think as she drove by that cemetery in the future. My hope was that the exercise and the cemetery, specifically, could serve as a lasting symbol, and that the other exercises she performed to mourn the loss would truly help her to bury her old identity so that she could come to see herself as recharged and strong, able and committed to seek out partners who were stable and who could love her back. Rather than seeing the prospect of new relationships as hopeless and bound to fail, I hoped that she would learn to see a new relationship in a broader perspective—as the birth of something new and full of potential. The truth is that a relationship between two people has a life of its own, and I wanted her to be able to create a life for her relationship that would be happy, healthy, and lasting.

Visit a Figurative Cemetery

If you prefer to do the burial exercise from the comfort of your own home, the exercise is going to require visualization. Find a quiet, peaceful part of the house and close your eyes. To set the scene, it will be helpful to imagine a cemetery and a group of people huddled around a tombstone. Imagine that everyone is wearing black clothing and bears sad, thoughtful expressions on their faces. The mourners are there to mark the passing of your old identity. They recognize that from this point forward, the "old you" will cease to exist. While they do feel the happiness that comes from knowing that your future relationships will be different—better—they came to the funeral to mourn the loss of your old identity. Because you can't hear what the leader of the group is saying as she gives the eulogy, fill in the blanks. Either say to yourself, or say out loud, the speech that accompanies the burial.

Create Your Own Cemetery

This is another way to conduct a burial ritual that doesn't involve a visit to the cemetery in the conventional sense. In this exercise, I want you to take a small box—it doesn't matter what kind—and place in it a reminder of your old relationship identity. This reminder could be a photo of you with an ex, the speech you gave to your baby picture, or some other reminder of the old you who spent all of those years repeating in vain. The final step is easy enough: Find a place to bury this box and place it in the ground. As you conduct this ceremony, feel free to make a speech about what the burial ritual means to you and what has died. This burial, like the two other rituals described in this section, can be a powerful experience, and I urge you to examine and try to connect with all of the feelings that wash over you as you go through this.

Light a Symbolic Candle

Finally, if none of the burial rituals described to this point resonate with you, you can forgo the cemetery imagery altogether. Try connecting with a different age-old and powerful symbol: lighting a candle. This ritual goes back centuries, and likely started in the Catholic Church when people lit candles in catacombs or in the tombs of martyrs to signify their connection with the deceased. Since then, lighting candles has taken on a similar meaning in the secular realm: You'll often see people who are gathered at a vigil—say, for the victims of the 9/11 attacks—lighting candles to signify their solidarity and hope. Mold the activity so that it's meaningful to you. Either take a trip to a nearby church (just about every church will have a quiet area with a collection of candles for this purpose) or designate a candle in your home to do the trick. After you light the candle, watch the flame for a few minutes and reflect on whatever—Renewal? Hope? Peaceful mourning?—it signifies to you.

THE TAKEAWAY

Giving up your old dysfunctional identity—that of someone who falls for men with whom you're ultimately incompatible—brings with it its own unique losses. This chapter is about mourning those losses by means of several exercises I urge you to conduct on your own. The exercises require you to visualize, recall some old memories, and rid your environment of toxic reminders as you fasten your seat belt for the full mourning experience. As you engage in these exercises, memories and feelings that have lain dormant for some time will likely reveal themselves. You will find that some of the reminders of the old you in those relationships will slip into your awareness like a gentle friend's embrace, while others will hit you like a Mack truck. Mourning the loss is both sweet and bitter, but the mourning will one day lead to something that sounds similar but is altogether more hopeful: a new day and a chance to do things differently from this point on.

SELF-EVALUATION
A Different Kind of Mourning

1. What is it like to mourn an old part of you? Does it feel good, strange, or a mix of both?

2. What prevented you from mourning the loss of your old identity until now? Why did you wait so long to do it?

3. Which mourning exercise do you most look forward to trying? Which do you least look forward to trying? (Hint: For the most significant growth, do the "least-looking-forward-to" exercise first.)

CHAPTER 14

The 800-Pound Gorilla

*Admitting the Problem and
Conducting Interviews*

THE COMPANY WE KEEP has a powerful impact on us—you can probably think of dozens of examples in your life that illustrate the truth of
this adage. Parents of teenage children are more cognizant of this fact
than anyone, which explains their vigilance in making sure that their
teenage children are socializing with the *right* children. Just as teenag-
ers' behavior is influenced by their peers, adults, too, are vulnerable to
a similar influence. You can easily be influenced by the relationship
behavior of your peers, whether you realize it or not.

If you are serious about calling it quits with your dysfunctional
relationship patterns, you will find that you can pave the way toward
goal achievement by socializing with role models who know how to
develop a healthy relationship. You can watch these couples as an
observer, almost like a scientist who monitors an animal's behavior in
its natural habitat. Specifically, when you observe healthy couples, you
can watch how successful couples manage the complex dynamics—
and occasional hiccups—that exist when two people create a union.
Most of all, you can see how good relationships prioritize giving and
receiving respect, and you can see how each partner's behavior provides constant evidence that they respect each other.

This chapter involves three simple parts: 1) admitting your problem, 2) conducting interviews with relationship mentors, and 3) reading the Serenity Prayer (which is really more of an affirmation than a prayer, as you'll soon see). I want you to roll up your sleeves and get to work on these simple steps right away!

Admitting the Problem

You're probably familiar with the Alcoholics Anonymous Twelve-Step terminology, repeated so often in popular films and television shows, beginning with the well-worn line, "Hello, my name is [so and so], and I'm an alcoholic." You may also have heard the expression that sums up the first of the twelve steps: admitting that you have a problem. The belief, according to the philosophy of the model, is that you cannot go about fixing a problem until you admit that there *is* a problem.

In picking up this book and sitting down to read it, you have already made a huge stride toward admitting your problem—repeating dysfunctional relationship patterns—to the most important person: yourself. I often spend a long time with clients in my office, trying to get them to the point where you have already gotten—where they're ready to pick up a book on the subject of their particular problem and figure out how to solve it.

Why the long struggle? Natural defense mechanisms kick in and people understandably want to minimize their problems. Because getting to the point of acknowledgment is often one of the longest legs of the journey toward actual change, you can take comfort in the fact that you are already well on your way. You're not lying around, wishing and hoping your relationships would get better—you're doing something proactive to get there!

Although I strongly believe that THE most important step in recovery is admitting to *yourself* that you have a problem with repeating bad relationship patterns, that's not all you have to do—you must also admit the problem to others. In fact, there's a reason why hundreds of thousands of alcoholics and addicts all over the world meet on any given day and sit in a circle to share their personal experiences and talk about their addictions and recoveries. The social support and public acknowledgment factors are critical. And while your problem is different from addiction or alcoholism, your own relationship recovery can benefit, in part, from what has worked well for so many alcoholics and addicts in recovery. In short, you need to admit the problem to others.

🔥 Hot Coals Task

I have marked certain exercises in this book as Hot Coals Tasks, meaning that completing them will likely require developing thicker *emotional* skin.

If you figure that others in your life already know that perhaps you're not the *greatest* at relationships and you think that's enough of an admission to others, unfortunately, you're not quite correct—I have a bit more work for you to do. This exercise is a more meaningful confession than you have likely made in the past to a friend or relative about your love life.

For this exercise, pick three people, representing a mix of family and friends. Please be kind to yourself here and choose people whom you trust and whom you know will show compassion toward you—you don't need anyone spewing unhelpful criticism about the romantic decisions you've made over the years. Instead, choose people who will listen and who care enough to help you solve your problem.

Once you've chosen your three individuals, I want you to speak to each of them within a few days—this step shouldn't take too long. The best way to conduct your admissions is to do them in person. If you must choose one of the three to conduct over the phone, I will give you a pass, but one is the limit!

Here's how you conduct the admission exercise:

- Start by explaining that you are reading a book to help you solve your problem with repeating relationships.
- Describe your relationship problem (the pattern you repeat and with whom you repeat it).
- Ask your confidant if he or she had previously noticed that you have this problem.
- Ask your confidant why he or she believes you have engaged in repeating behavior while others may not have had such difficulty with relationships.

In reviewing the different steps involved in admitting the problem to someone, you might ask yourself why the last step is necessary—why it's important to hear his or her thoughts about why you repeated patterns in the past. After all, chances are that your confidant isn't a licensed mental health professional, so why ask for his or her analysis? Simply put, because it's a crucial building block of recovery to accept vulnerability and to learn how to listen to those you trust.

After you conduct your interviews with your confidants and have spoken with them about your problem, I want you to follow up with a quick writing exercise:

- Pull out the Changes Journal you started earlier.
- Write down what each of your confidants said to you.
- Describe what it was like to admit your problem to each confidant.

Engaging in these exercises isn't necessarily easy or even comfortable. While I know that some of these behaviors may strike you as a little odd or too contrived, I also know that exercises such as these actually work—they help the RRs I treat in my office on a daily basis.

Because it may be difficult to picture exactly what the admission step looks like when carried out in real life, an example follows.

Remember Daphne, the emotional chaser of men who always managed to push her away? Here you can get a sense of what admitting the problem to a girlfriend was like for her. Daphne picked a day to meet her friend when Daphne didn't have to work, and suggested they meet at her favorite outdoor coffee shop on a tree-lined street near her house. In her session with me, Daphne filled me in on the details of what she said during her admission process.

> *So, I'm meeting with a therapist to talk about some of my past relationships, and one of the things I'm supposed to do as a part of the program is to tell a friend what's going on. Basically, I have a problem with relationships. I know you know that, but I'm supposed to say it anyhow. For whatever reason—and actually, I'm kind of getting a better idea of those reasons—I keep repeating the same patterns and getting into relationships with the wrong guys. I decided I'm sick and tired of feeling like this in my relationships, so I am trying all these different things to break the cycle. I can imagine what's coming next, because you've known me for so long, but I'm supposed to ask: Did you ever notice that I have a problem with relationships?*

You can tell that conducting the exercise was a little strange for Daphne. Sure, she was accustomed to seeing her friend frequently on a casual basis, but meeting with her to conduct the exercise felt different—more formal. Her response reflected my intention for her: to try something unfamiliar and make an announcement. I don't need to tell you how Daphne's friend responded to her last question, because you probably already know how transparent we can be to those who know us best.

Now that you understand how the whole admission process works, it's time to put the rubber to the road and start your own engine. Ladies, prepare for your first (and then, of course, second and third) admission!

Relationship Mentors

Now it's time to try another exercise that is a bit more enjoyable, and certainly simple: conducting interviews. The point of the interview is for you to gain a clear understanding of how others manage good relationships and for you to distinguish between the characteristics you prioritize in looking for a relationship and the process other people used to find a compatible partner.

For this exercise, I want you to mentally scan your entire social circle and come up with three couples that you feel have a solid, long-term relationship. Remember, no relationship is perfect, so simply come up with three couples who have made it work for a while and who seem to still like each other!

Once you've identified three couples, pretend you are a novice journalist chasing after a hot scoop. In preparation, make a mental note of a few simple questions you are going to ask the couples as you interview them. My guess is that once you get going, you will probably want to throw in a few of your own questions, too. The questions are basic, designed for you to uncover the secrets of their romantic success so that this insight can inform your own partner selection in the future. There is no particular order to stick to for asking questions. Keep in mind that the point is to capture the essence of how they found their partner rather than to remember the questions verbatim:

- What first drew you to your partner?
- Before you met him or her, what qualities were you looking for in a long-term partner?
- Did you ever have any bad romantic experiences before you met the one who would become your partner? If so, how did those experiences impact your partner selection process?
- In general, what do you believe the qualities are that make for a successful romantic relationship?
- How could you tell that your current partner had these traits?

- What are the different ways that each of you offers emotional support to the other?

Conducting interviews and getting feedback from individuals who know how to "do" relationships well will provide you with insights that you can use as you reset your relationship switches and approach your future relationships from a healthy perspective.

The Serenity Prayer

Let's discuss using the Serenity Prayer, a tool as important to recovery as a hammer is to a tool set. The popularity of this prayer is an obvious testament to its wisdom—it's recited at thousands of twelve-step meetings every day across the country and around the world. The prayer is ubiquitous enough that you may have already heard it. Regardless of your beliefs about God, I hope you can appreciate the value of this prayer. One of the most common obstacles reported by clients who first learn about the prayer centers around the idea of invoking God, and the prayer's association with organized religion. While some of you may proudly identify with a given religion or spiritual orientation, others may feel reluctant to adopt a religious or spiritual practice. I have written this book to help you recover from repeating dysfunctional relationship patterns and do not espouse any religious or nonreligious agenda. Overall, my belief is that the Serenity Prayer bears profound wisdom and should be respected for its core tenets—not discarded simply because you may not identify with any particular religion or may not believe in God yourself. If you have a problem with the use of "God," omit it in your usage of the prayer. Whether it's new or familiar to you, read it and breathe it in slowly, as if it's the first time you've come across it. *God, grant me the serenity to accept the things I cannot change, the courage to change the things I can, and the wisdom to know the difference.*

What's interesting about the prayer itself is that it was originally designed for individuals recovering from drug or alcoholic addiction, but its use has expanded over time to include people suffering from a variety of problems—codependence, overeating, and so on. Rest assured that the prayer applies to the problem of romantic repeating. These exercises are intended to help you gain insight into the characteristics of your partners that can change, and to distinguish them from those characteristics that probably won't. If you read and reread the prayer, you can continue to see new incarnations of its wisdom and its application to the problem of repeating toxic relationship patterns.

We are using trial and error to determine what works for you as you morph from an RR into a woman who has control over her romantic destiny. Open your eyes to all the tools for change, take what works, and leave behind what doesn't. Never forget that you are in the driver's seat when it comes to the exercises you engage in to solidify and seal your own relationship recovery. It's your life, your relationships are your own, and your romantic future is yours to custom-design!

THE TAKEAWAY

In this chapter, you learned about two new exercises, admitting the problem and conducting interviews, and were introduced to a coping tool that has proven useful for thousands of recovering individuals: the Serenity Prayer. These exercises are behaviors that are critical to your own relationship recovery, sending a direct signal to your identity and announcing that a change in how you approach relationships is coming soon. The more seriously you take the exercises and actually use these tools, the brighter the signal will become. As you go through these changes, remember to document everything—any random thoughts or epiphanies—in your Changes Journal. At some point in the future, when repeating is long behind you and a new beau waits on the horizon, you will appreciate having this document as a reminder of your old relationship ways. At that point, you will look back and marvel at the fact that you ever settled for such unfulfilling relationships.

SELF-EVALUATION
Derive Strength from the Positive

1. What are the characteristics of the people you will choose to admit the problem to that will make you feel comfortable to conduct the exercise with them?

2. Why do you imagine I asked you to conduct the admission exercise with more than one person? (Hint: think about the legitimacy of a doctor's second opinion.)

3. When you imagine what the couples you interview will say in terms of which qualities they prioritized in choosing a long-term partner, what are a few of the qualities you imagine will come up?

4. Had you ever fully read the Serenity Prayer before? If so, have you ever used it? If not, how will you use it in the future? Write it down? Verbally recite it?

CHAPTER 15

A New Beginning

Fresh Techniques to Ensure Healthy Relationships

YOU CROSSED A MAJOR threshold as you worked through the exercises in the previous chapter. At this point, you're like a marathon runner who's just practiced her last long run before the day of the big race. You are now ready to learn the five techniques that will help you do away with your dysfunctional pattern-repeating tendencies once and for all so that you can find the man who is a good match for you!

This chapter will focus on one simple message: the repeating is over.

The exercises presented in this chapter will help banish, once and for all, the old you—the one who repeated. These aren't disposable techniques, to be used once and then discarded. Instead, they can provide a regular and reliable resource as you morph from repeater into a healthy lover. Please trust me: the more you employ these techniques, the more you will strengthen your resolve to do things differently in your next relationship, which—news flash!—could be one that lasts.

Affirmations

Whether you know it or not, affirmations are all around you—in a wise proverb embroidered on a pillow, in a prayer someone uses prior to a meal or at the end of the day, or even in a group cheer during a huddle at a football game. Affirmations are important because they remind each of us of the goals we hold for a particular area of our lives. Some people's affirmations may focus on winning; others may center on gaining wisdom and strength. For you, my relationship-repeating friend, the focus must be on ending the repetition cycle and approaching relationships from a brand-new perspective.

The reason to incorporate affirmations into your daily routine is simple: You must be clear and focused, and you must also be a friend to yourself as you face potential obstacles on your way toward change that sticks. The latter point is crucial, because the road to changing your romantic identity is flanked by ditches and invariably includes a few sharp turns. Affirmations can help to counter some of the thoughts and feelings that act as change's enemy, those that keep you frozen in place as you try to move on and grow. You probably know what I'm talking about—the voice in the back of your head that sometimes tells you it's too hard to change or that change isn't even possible. Today, you may be feeling a little more positive about what lies ahead on the horizon, believing that you can truly kick the repetition habit and find a partner who is actually good for you. Yet you might have a day in the near future when your mood is down and you find yourself entertaining a lingering negative thought like "Who am I kidding? Why would things be any different next time?"

These thoughts—the things you tell yourself in your head without actually saying anything out loud—are what we in the mental health field call "self-talk." In other words, it's the running dialogue we hear chattering in our mind throughout the day as we go about our tasks and activities. In response to an event that just happened to us, self-talk can be negative (you say to yourself, "There you go again, you idiot") or positive (you say to yourself, "Just blow it off, at least you did your best").

I can't stress enough the importance of the tone of your self-talk: This inner dialogue we have with ourselves largely determines how we feel. The goal is to learn to use affirmations that encourage positive self-talk. As you rid yourself of your old identity as an RR, you must find affirmations to remind you that change is possible and that you can have better relationships in the future. When you have a lonely day or perhaps a dicey romantic encounter with a potential suitor, using affirmations will help you to stay focused and positive.

Again, there is no correct way to employ affirmations—you find what works for you through trial and error. While some find that spoken affirmations are most helpful (reciting aloud a one- or two-sentence statement), others may find that putting pen to paper works best (writing the same affirmation in a journal or even using scratch paper at work on a regular basis). Following is an example of the way that my client Valerie used affirmations to help her to stop repeating. In a session with me, she explained how she added a unique twist that fit naturally for her.

For me, saying something out loud didn't really work, so I tried writing something down. Actually, I wrote a couple things on some sticky notes and I keep one on the bathroom mirror and another by my bed. On one, I wrote "No more repeating, no more drama." On the second one, I wrote, "You will find love that's good." I don't know why, but they really help me—I find myself smiling and nodding a little every time I see them, and sort of regaining more solid footing when I'm starting to go to a darker mental place.

Valerie had wholeheartedly grasped the point of the affirmations—to make you feel positive, centered, and in control. She first tried to do a verbal affirmation but found that something written suited her better. You will figure out on your own what works best for you. Remember, when you speak or write your affirmations, try several to figure out which ones resonate with you.

Before we move on, I will give you a few examples that you could use as a foundation for crafting your own affirmation.

- The next time I fall in love, I am going to . . .
- I have learned that I need to . . .
- Dating is risky business, which is why I need to . . .
- I know that I am special, and I need a man to . . .

You get the picture. Find one or more affirmations that work for you, and use them daily.

🔥 *Hot Coals Task*

While the previous exercise required you to be a chef of sorts and create your affirmations from scratch, this next exercise comes with a ready-made recipe; all you need to do is apply what you're given. To start, if I were to ask you what you associate with the word "vow"—in other words, what first pops into your head when you hear that term—my guess is you would conjure thoughts of marriage or a wedding ceremony. In fact, the tradition of wedding ceremonies has, for years and across cultures, included the exchange of vows because they can neatly, concisely, and with seriousness communicate a message. Vows aren't silly—they're serious, heartfelt, and convey our loftiest aspirations. As we're borrowing from multiple disciplines and experiences in an effort to take the best and leave the rest, we are going to take vows from their traditional context and apply them to our mission of stopping the repetition cycle and finding a relationship that lasts.

As you read the vows that follow, say them out loud so you can hear yourself saying them. By doing this, you will send yourself the direct message that you are committing to new and healthier relationship behavior. If you've ever attended a Buddhist chant group, you heard a group of people reciting the same few sentences over and over. To the bystander, such chanting may seem odd or even useless. However, the chanter can allow herself to get lost in the predictable rhythm of the chant and connect with the goal she has set for herself. Similarly, you should connect with your vows and what they have to say about relationships.

Each vow should become your friend and confidant, your teacher and guide. Recite these regularly and you will begin to hear the positive self-talk in the back of your mind adopt a more assertive voice over the negative version, thereby ushering you toward men who are more compatible with you. In addition, these vows will direct you toward behavior that is self-protective rather than self-destructive.

Ten Vows

1. I will stop repeating bad relationship patterns.
2. I will respect myself in my relationships.
3. I will verbally express my thoughts and feelings when I feel disrespected or unhappy in my relationship.
4. I will not allow abuse of any kind.
5. I will be honest with myself about what I want from a relationship.
6. I will tell my partner what I want to see in my future (commitment, marriage, children, and so on).
7. I will express my feelings when necessary and sit with my feelings when necessary.
8. I will not try to change my partner.
9. I will end my relationship if I am being mistreated or if my primary needs are not being met.
10. I will break the cycle of Relationship Repetition Syndrome.

I have used this list of vows with my clients and have found them to be incredibly helpful in breaking the repetition cycle. However, the exercise is not set in stone—you can write a new list if you'd like, or simply subtract a few and insert some of your own. The ultimate goal is this: Use your vows on a daily basis and recite them out loud or write them down. While you are in the throes of a true transition— say, for example, morphing from an RR into someone who is capable of mutual, full-fledged love—you will benefit from using these vows daily, perhaps even a few times per day. As you begin to move further along the road toward changing your approach to relationships, you may find that you don't need to return to them as frequently.

Visualizing a New Kind of Romance

When I say "visualization," I'm not talking about hypnosis or simply closing your eyes and wishing things were different. It's a technique that asks you to consciously, and with detail, create a different reality in your mind. Visualization is helpful in teaching you mental flexibility, and will help send a message to your instincts that you're shutting the door to unkind situations that you have heretofore accepted.

The following series of prompts asks you to visualize two different situations: In the first group of exercises, you'll visualize yourself actively rejecting the type of partner you would have pursued in the past; in the second group, you'll visualize a new kind of partner. Let yourself flesh out these imaginary scenes with details, emotions, facial expressions, settings, and so on. Try to spend at least a couple of minutes on each prompt.

Visualizing Yourself

1. Recall an experience you had with an ex-partner who upset you. Did he betray you? Say something hurtful? Push you away? Now recall how you reacted. Odds are that you would do something differently if you could go back and relive that moment now. This revised version of what happened is what you should visualize. What would your posture be like? What would you say? Imagine that he responds to you in a way that might be typical of him, and visualize how you would reply.

2. Now imagine that a new man in the future says or does something that you feel is disrespectful. Once you've conjured this image, put yourself in the picture and imagine your internal reaction. Do you feel hurt? Angry? Insecure? In your mind, make sure you have a vivid picture of the actual location (in a restaurant? on the street?), what you are wearing, and the time of day it occurs. Now visualize how you respond to him.

3. Finally, take the last scenario you visualized—the one in which a new man really upset you and you stood up for yourself—and imagine telling one of your good friends about it. Who would you call to recount the experience? Visualize yourself picking up the phone, hearing it ringing, and picture the expressions on your face as you recount the experience to your friend and where in the conversation your voice picks up speed, gets louder, or catches in your throat. What's the first thing you say to your friend in your visualization? How does your friend respond? What kind of conclusion do the two of you reach about the situation before you hang up?

Candice, the client who repeatedly found herself with men who cheated, told me that after she tried these visualization techniques on her own, she felt little rushes of adrenaline and a sense of satisfaction. Here, she talks about her first visualization experience:

> *I visualized the time when I organized a weekend trip for my boyfriend and I, and he put it off over and over again until I just canceled it. When that happened, I took it really personally but tried not to show him how upset I was. When I visualized a new man doing the same thing—well, let's just say I spoke up to him. I told him straight: I want to be with someone who wants to be with me. If you don't, I said to him, that's fine, but in that case I'll certainly be moving on and looking for someone who wants to actually spend time with me. I can't go back in time and say that to him, but as it turns out, acting it out in your mind is definitely the next best thing.*

This shows how empowering visualization can be. It's a chance to rewrite the script so you end up with someone you want, and who simply wants to be with you, too.

Now you get to move on to the next visualization, in which you play magician and create a new (albeit imaginary) man in your life. In this exercise, try to avoid focusing all your energy on building a handsome man with eyes of a particular color and a wide smile of perfect white teeth. Remember that these characteristics are external and have nothing to do with finding emotional compatibility—your long-term goal as you work to break the repetition cycle. Sure, as you conduct the next exercises, it's okay to imagine someone attractive, but you should keep in mind that the *emotional* fantasy is what we're aiming for here.

Visualizing a New Partner

1. Imagine that you are celebrating your next birthday, and you come home to find that your new boyfriend has organized a surprise for you. Picture the place where you currently live. Visualize what the surprise is, and imagine him planning it (making whatever phone calls he needed to make and any other challenges he may have faced in putting the surprise together). As you conduct this visualization exercise, imagine the look on his face when he surprises you. At first, it may be difficult to visualize a man you haven't met. If this feels like a challenge, choose a random image from a magazine or a face that flashes across the television screen (try to avoid using the face of someone you actually know). But remember, this exercise is not about the man's appearance!

2. Next, imagine that you have had a terrible day and call a new boyfriend in the afternoon to tell him about it and to receive some comfort and reassurance. Draw up a rough sketch of what happened to make the day so rotten. Now visualize that you are crying, feeling overwhelmed with both sadness and anger as a result

of what's transpired. Imagine that your boyfriend's voice is calm and reassuring, and that he tells you he is hanging up the phone and coming to meet you where you are. You go to answer the door when he arrives, and visualize him hugging you and then holding you for several minutes. Try to picture what he says to you in this moment as he asks you questions about what happened and asks what he can do to make you feel better.

3. Finally, imagine that you have recently met a new promising love prospect but have had fleeting anxiety as you begin a new relationship. At times, you wonder if he might be *too* nice or sweet for you, if he might be too different from you, or if you might not be ready for a relationship. Given your insecurities, you tell your best friend about your anxieties. She assures you that these are normal anxieties and advises you to give it some time to see if things work out. Visualize having a conversation with the new man in your life and telling him that you need to move slowly because you have been hurt in the past. Pause here for a moment and think about how you would choose your words. Visualize that his response is completely sensitive—he doesn't get turned off after you have shared details about your past. I want you to visualize that he listens to what you have to say, gives you a warm hug, and says he understands and wants to do what he can to help. How do you respond?

These visualization exercises may feel similar to daydreams, except that they require more awareness and control. You can use these exercises again and again, and can change the wording or events in the exercises as you see fit. After working through these exercises you should see the point: To be happy in a relationship, your partner needs to focus on your emotional needs and care about how you feel.

THE TAKEAWAY

In this chapter, you learned about several helpful techniques for stepping off the relationship repetition merry-go-round for good. Specifically, you learned about affirmations, vows, and visualizations, which all help to rewrite the knee-jerk reactions that guided you in the past toward some not-so-compatible partners, freeing you today to gravitate toward men who fit you well. In reading about Valerie's and Candice's experiences with the affirmation and visualization exercises, you saw examples that illustrate the power of the imagination. My hope is that you saw how much fun exercises can be when they put you in a position of empowerment and control. In conducting the exercises, you are engaging in behavior that helps to cement the fact that your repeating days are over and that a "new you" is developing in its place. You will see in the next chapter that ridding yourself of your repeating identity leaves just enough space for the birth of a new relationship identity— one that is ready to move on, find meaningful love, and put the past and all its destructive repetition behind you.

SELF-EVALUATION
Exercises for Your Spirit

1. Which type of affirmation will you most likely use: verbal, written, or a mix of both? Why?

2. Go back and take a quick look at the ten vows exercise. Which vow do you believe is the most powerful?

3. Which visualization exercise did you like the best? What did you like about the exercise? How did you feel after you completed it?

4. In one of the visualization exercises you just finished, I asked you to imagine yourself upset and crying, and to imagine your boyfriend comforting you, holding you, and listening to you as long as necessary. What was it like for you to imagine this?

CHAPTER 16

Changing Your Emotional Scenery

Different Ways to Do the Same Old Things

YOU ARE NOW EQUIPPED with ample tools to stop the repetition process. Admittedly, this will be no easy feat, given that for years you've been operating in a fixed romantic gear. While I am optimistic about your ability to survive and exceed this challenge, you must fully understand the need to recalibrate your romantic gears.

A history of unfulfilling relationships indicates that something was off in the way you approached men and relationships in the past, almost in the way that a car's repeated breakdowns indicates there is a particular mechanical error. When it comes to ending a cycle of repetition, simply stopping the pattern is not enough: now you need to create a new identity. In order to do that, you must fix your own (romantic) mechanical errors so that your relationship gears function smoothly and effectively.

Think about it: For years you engaged in repeating behavior with incompatible men, not because you liked repeating, but because you, like other RRs, probably got stuck in a particular behavior pattern with men and had difficulty getting out of that gear. Changing how you approach men and relationships is difficult because who you choose as a partner stems from how you feel about yourself, how fulfilled you feel in your life overall, and how good you expect your life to be. When you stop repeating, you kill off the old identity of a woman who fails in relationships and give life to a new identity as a woman who knows what she wants and gets what she needs.

Here, we'll take a look at the concepts and behaviors that will create this identity shift so that a "new you" fills the existing hole that was left when you abandoned the repeating "you." While the previous chapter focused on the negative (getting rid of the toxic repetition), this chapter will focus on the positive (rebuilding a new identity in its place). In this chapter, you'll learn a few techniques that will help you usher in a new, fresh approach to love—one that isn't weary, bitter, or dejected. You will soon find that engaging in these techniques will lift your spirits, remind you that change is possible, and develop a foundation from which you can build a happy, lasting relationship.

How Not *to Lose Yourself in a Relationship*

When you are romantically involved, you undoubtedly put a lot of thought into the relationship. It's common to think about your partner often, evaluate how the relationship is going, and wonder about the future of the relationship. However, as natural and easy as it is to focus on the relationship with your partner, you should be ever mindful of the relationship you're conducting on the side: the relationship with yourself. I frame this concept to my clients in the following way: In a relationship, you aren't monogamous; you're polygamous-monogamous. In other words, you get two relationships for the price of one.

Every human being—at least those not residing under a rock—has heard an aphorism along the lines of, "You must first love yourself in order to love somebody else." Although the concept of first loving yourself as a foundation for loving someone else is so ubiquitous that it's been memorialized in popular songs (a la "The Greatest Love of All," most famously sung by Whitney Houston), you may not have examined how its advice applies to you.

One way to make sure that you don't lose yourself in your relationship is to focus on developing and cultivating yourself, making sure that you are whole on your own. Remember what I have emphasized all along: RRs who lose themselves in relationships often, unsurprisingly, forget about other areas of their lives. Hence, the forgotten areas of the RRs' lives wither from neglect like an unwatered plant.

The Four-Burner Theory: Happiness Requires More Than a Romantic Relationship

Your love life will benefit from your regularly stepping back and looking at the big picture of your life—one in which your romantic relationships are merely one part as opposed to the entire foundation on which your happiness depends. In working with RRs, I have found that the most succinct way to illustrate the proper balance between the amount of time spent obsessing about your relationship and the amount of time spent thinking about the other areas of your life is to use an analogy, and mine involves a basic four-top stove. Just as a stove has four burners, your life should have several different components as well. Let's say that on one burner you have a relationship cooking, on another you have your work or career, and perhaps percolating on the remaining burners you have hobbies, friendships, or whatever else defines you and commands attention in your day-to-day life. I explain to my clients that their past relationships were problematic, in part, because RRs tend to lose themselves focusing too much on that single burner and fail to pay attention to what is boiling over elsewhere. Again, this makes sense: if you're in an unfulfilling and difficult relationship, you don't have a lot of energy for much else.

All this means is that since you're now recovering from relationship repetition, you are going to have more time because you'll be spending less time repeating. Now is the perfect time to get something cooking on the other burners so that you don't risk focusing too much on your relationships in the future—you need a balance, after all. But you'll have to make some changes right away to signal this transition. Here, I have isolated four behaviors that will help you shift your identity from RR to someone who is approaching relationships—and the stovetop of her life—in an entirely new way.

FOUR IDENTITY SHIFTERS:
THE GOAL IS TO USE ALL FOUR BURNERS
1. Symbolize the birth of your new identity
2. Turn on a new burner by trying something new
3. Create new daily routines
4. Give back to the community

🔥 Hot Coals Task

The first step in creating a new relationship identity is to find something that symbolizes a new beginning.

Identity Shifter Number One:
Symbolize the Birth of Your New Identity

It could be a plant, a framed photograph that suggests the birth or beginning of something, or something you made to indicate that you are now creating a new part of yourself. Using a living organism to symbolize this new beginning is a good idea and can be done easily with plants, but you can choose something else if you'd like. I urge the RRs I treat to invest in plants, trees, or flowers, and am never surprised by their later reports that the leafy companions helped remind them of the possibility for growth and for a fresh beginning. Whatever you choose to symbolize your new beginning, make sure that you keep it somewhere where you can see it several times during the day.

Identity Shifter Number Two:
Turn on a New Burner by Trying Something New

All RRs have fallen into their common predicament because, in more ways than one, they're frozen in a fixed way of behaving, almost like mechanical beings who gravitated toward the wrong partners. Accordingly, this part of the recovery process will focus on getting unfrozen and trying new things.

Some RRs have tripped into the well of relationship repetition because, in part, they have become overly sheltered. It's not just that they've been stuck in a go-nowhere relationship and felt unhappy because their basic emotional needs have gone unmet; other factors have led to their isolation as well. It's often the case that their social group has become stagnant, with no new faces joining the circle, which can mean that they aren't connected to a diverse group of people and personalities.

Our first step: I want you to add a new social activity or hobby to your life so that you get something else, besides a relationship, cooking on your stove. Keep in mind that you should not approach this task with the goal that may reflexively pop into your mind—meeting a new man. I'd like you to try to have the opposite intention. The goal is to put yourself out there for the sake of your own development, so for the moment, table the search to meet someone new and the exclusive focus on relationships. You'll find that heating up one or more additional burners, likely long cold from disuse, will serve to deepen and sustain the happiness and fulfillment you experience in your day-to-day life.

When it comes to the social activities or hobbies you could embark upon, the possibilities are endless. First, go back to Chapter 10 and take a look at the section about your basic personality style. What did you determine: Are you more of an introvert or extrovert? The answer to this question is important because it can help you narrow down the types of activities that will lead to the most growth. For example, if you are an introvert and naturally gravitate toward solitary activities, you probably need to join a social group that will get you out of the house, introduce you to new people, and get you more connected to a social community. On the other hand, if you are a total extrovert, spending time with others is hardly your problem. For this reason, you probably need to develop a hobby or activity that encourages greater introspection and allows for self-soothing. Keeping in mind that you might need to become a little more comfortable spending time with *just yourself* and learning to feel a little less dependent on others to feel good, you should choose an activity you can do on your own or with only a small group of people.

Examples of solitary or low-key social activities if you're more extroverted:

- Enroll in an art or cooking class at a local community college.
- Learn how to crochet, knit, quilt, embroider, or do other needlework.
- Take a foreign language class.

Examples of more social activities for those who are introverted:

- Join or start a monthly game night.
- Find a book club.
- Start a rotating potluck dinner club in which the cuisine and location changes monthly.
- Go to *www.Meetup.com* and find a group in your area that matches your interests (on the site you'll find everything from groups who try new restaurants to those who watch and discuss movies or are learning a language together).

Finding the activity that's right for you will not necessarily happen immediately; you may have to go through some trial and error to find the right fit. Don't be afraid to put in the legwork: Ask around at work, send a mass e-mail to your social circle, or look online to find an activity that matches your values and interests. Or start with a type of activity you want to pursue and inquire at relevant locations about potential activities. I know of craft stores, for example, that sponsor monthly events, libraries that have various types of gatherings and classes, and so on. If you give this task some thought, you'll eventually come up with something that appeals to you.

Stretching yourself at this point of your journey is a necessary part of the recovery process. Simply stopping repeating isn't enough to allow you to find a better relationship—you must actually approach your future relationships from a totally different perspective, and part of that requires you to make some changes in yourself. I've noticed while watching recovering RRs that creating nourishing elements on a few other burners helps to establish a better mind frame from which to meet someone new and then later from which to maintain a relationship. With some effort and perseverance, you can create the identity of someone happy, healthy, and ready to offer herself as a solid partner in a lasting relationship.

Identity Shifter Number Three:
Create New Daily Routines

Too easily, we get caught up in routines and go about our day with a shocking lack of awareness. For example, you may pick up an organic yogurt and banana for breakfast in the morning but smoke a cigarette just before you get to work. You may swear off your ex-boyfriend but habitually check your text messages to see if he has contacted you. It never fails: We, as humans, are dreadfully capable of inconsistencies and contradictions, even in our ingrained routines. The goal is to become more aware and discerning of our motivations and behaviors so that we link what we want with what we are setting ourselves up for.

I'm sure you can relate to people who say they always find themselves driving or walking the same way to work, picking up a coffee or latte from the exact same coffee shop, or patronizing the same gym they've gone to for years, even if it leaves something to be desired and is the only one they've been to in town. Some of us may go out socially on exactly the same day every week, only see one type of movie ad infinitum, and eat the same few things for dinner week in and week out. Creating a new, more balanced identity involves announcing to yourself and the world that you have packed your things and left your comfort zone, and that you'll be creating a new identity along the way.

REMEMBERING OUR MODEL FOR CHANGE

Making changes in your daily routine is a terrific and effective way to align your behavior with the additional insight you've accumulated so far. Remember the model for change I introduced earlier?

Insight + Behavior Change = Identity Change

It is the addition of new behaviors to your newfound insight that creates a real change in your identity—in short, the way you operate in the world and, particularly, your relationships!

Following our prescription for change, you are going to make some small changes to your daily routine. Ideally, you'll make one change each in your morning, midday, and evening routines. Go ahead and pull out your Changes Journal, and get ready to jot down a few notes.

MORNING ROUTINE

Write down all of the little routines you have in the morning as you get ready for your day. This could include lingering in bed for a few minutes as you wake up, showering, putting on your makeup, feeding the cat or dog, and grabbing something quick for breakfast. Next, I want you to write down all of the little things you do once you leave the house for work. (Of course, if you work at home, your job for this part of the exercise will include only the first part). Once you have your list, you are going to add something new to it, some small behavior that will positively add to your day and nourish your spirit at the same time. Take a look at how Penelope performed this exercise, and you will get a better idea of what I mean. She explained that it was the slightest change that made the difference, and she wore a proud smile as she recounted the details.

When I looked at my routine, I realized that my morning was just a manic quest to get out of the house and get to work. I started thinking about ways I could actually take a minute to breathe in the morning so my day didn't start out in such a frantic trance. I basically kept everything the same except that I decided to make it a point to sit for five quiet minutes and eat my breakfast instead of forcing yogurt down my throat in the car on the way to work. I really liked the change. I now go through the mail while I eat or look at my daily planner and think about what I have to do that day. It's nice. I feel like things in my life are really calm and together in these moments, and I'd definitely rather set the tone for my day on a peaceful note than on a hectic one.

Penelope found that recovery from unconsciously repeating toxic relationship patterns required her to look at other areas of her life that needed a little tune-up as well. It occurred to her after making this small change in her morning routine that more calm and collected moments could have allowed her to sort through her own thoughts when she'd been caught in the centrifuge of dysfunctional relationships in the past. In the end, it occurred to her that had she been better at slowing down all along, she may have been much less likely to brush aside the feelings that went along with her destructive relationships.

MIDDAY ROUTINE

As you did with the morning exercise, make a list of habits that you've developed over your lunch hour, or simply the hour or two in the middle of your day. Are you someone who grabs lunch and eats at your desk, or do you always run down to the café across the street? Are you able to make lunch in your own kitchen? Perhaps you usually have lunch a few days per week with friends. Obviously there's nothing wrong with these activities, but you must tweak or add one midday routine to facilitate an identity shift. Perhaps it's time to consider adding a ten-minute walk into your lunch hour, scheduling a quick manicure on the first of every month, or bringing some gym clothes to work and slipping in twenty minutes on the treadmill once or twice per week. I suggest looking for activities that center on themes of nature, touch, or exercising your body, all of which directly relate to how you feel physically and emotionally.

EVENING ROUTINE

There's little doubt about a universal temptation after a long day of work: plopping down onto the couch and turning on the television. I'll readily admit that I have a love/hate relationship with what I affectionately call the boob tube. But the not-so-secret truth is that sitting and watching television is one of the most passive activities a human being can engage in. I strongly recommend allowing yourself no more than one hour per day. If you're a current tube-o-phile (and find yourself regularly logging more than three hours in front of the small screen each day), I guarantee that you will see improvement in your emotional life once you curb your TV time.

When you think of your evening routine, I'm guessing that watching television is only one part of it. Write down the typical behaviors that you engage in from approximately 7:00 in the evening until you go to bed. Delve into the details: among these activities, you might change your clothes, throw something together for dinner, check e-mails, talk on the phone, read a magazine or newspaper, prepare for bed, and set the alarm for the next day. Now I want you to add something new to the list.

In line with the ultimate nourishment goal—engaging in activities that make you feel good, relax you, and restore a sense of balance to your mind—come up with one or two activities you can add to your evening that you would look forward to as your day winds down. My client Maryann told me about a change she made that she fell in love with almost instantly.

> *I made a couple of small changes to my routine at night, but the one I have come to appreciate the most sounds like the most minor thing: changing gyms. It's been really nice to go somewhere new where I see a whole set of new faces. I've said hello to a few new people, but it's more the fact that everything doesn't feel exactly the same as it had for so long. After making this change, I started to think that maybe I'd make a change like this every year or so, just to freshen things up once in a while.*

To hear how this minor change ended up lifting Maryann's spirits every day was heartwarming, because she got the point and embraced it. In considering the idea that she should perhaps make a small, seemingly insignificant change to her general routine every year perfectly captured the essence of the four-burner theory. Just as you occasionally check the size of the flame underneath a pot cooking on the stove, you must also check the metaphorical burners in your life to see if they need a little adjustment. In other words, fulfillment requires constant vigilance and regular recalibration, because different things make you happy at different points in your life.

Identity Shifter Number Four: Give Back to the Community

As you recover from relationship repetition, finding a way to give back to the community will help you invest your time in something meaningful, since you're no longer wasting your time with relationships that aren't going anywhere. In addition, getting involved in the community in a charitable sense will help you to get out of your own head and avoid overthinking the negatives in your own life. Remember the charity inventory that you took in Chapter 12? Now you understand why we spent time taking inventory of this area of your life. You will find that giving is healing. It is important to get involved with a group that *gives back to the community,* because doing so will put you in contact with other givers and help you to consider the place where you live in a larger context. After all, it's a global world these days, and we must become increasingly aware of the bigger picture outside of our own specific, local circumstances.

There are numerous ways to get connected with the community in which you live. You might want to join a church or perhaps change churches, as churches or other spiritual organizations often organize regular charitable events. If church isn't for you, try another volunteer organization that represents a cause that means something to you. Always go back to the basics when you try to navigate your way through a problem: ask yourself what you care about and what your strengths are. For you, perhaps this is a politically oriented group, or it could be an organization that reaches out to the homeless, to youth, or to animals. If you need some prompting to find the right fit for you, go back to Chapter 10 and look at your inventory responses. Most medium and large cities have general volunteer organizations through which you can research several different kinds of charitable opportunities in one place, either in the organizations' offices or on their websites.

A quick check-in: Are you surprised that most of this chapter made little reference to romantic relationships? You shouldn't be. What I want you to completely internalize is the point that part of the reason your relationships have gotten off-track over the years is because you probably lost a part of yourself somewhere along the way. Remember, you need to keep tabs on the things that make you *you,* or you can get lost without even knowing it at the time. The way you hold on to yourself and become a healthy 50 percent of a romantic relationship is to continue to cultivate yourself—and keep something cooking on all four burners, rather than focusing too much on a relationship with the distorted belief that it will be enough to fulfill you.

THE TAKEAWAY

This chapter's main purpose was to show you what comes after you stop repeating: You must replace the old with something new. As such, this chapter showed you ways to help create an identity shift in which you come to see yourself as a changed person, one who would never repeat but who takes a proactive and holistic approach to finding fulfillment. Concepts such as polygamous monogamy and the four-burner theory show that you must be fulfilled on your own in order to find and maintain a lasting relationship. I always say that a happy relationship houses two people who are individually happy and whole. Finally, the chapter introduced you to four simple behaviors—behaviors I call Identity Shifters—that you can engage in to develop the identity of someone who knows what she wants, how to get it, and how to hold on to it.

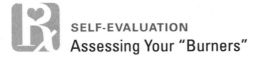

SELF-EVALUATION
Assessing Your "Burners"

1. In terms of symbols that indicate a new beginning, why do you imagine that plants are particularly effective?

2. I trust that you will make several changes to the different parts of your daily routine—morning, midday, and evening. What is one addition you can make right away and with little difficulty?

3. Go back to my four-burner theory. What is one burner, besides your relationships, that you already know needs a tune-up?

PART V

Wearing Your New Relationship Identity and Moving On

CHAPTER 17

Building (or Rebuilding) Your Relationship

Try Out Your New POV

YOU. HAVE. ALREADY. STARTED. TO. CHANGE. Now, give me just a moment before you dismiss my dramatic pronouncement and send the book flying across the room. Having reached this point in the book, you have no doubt gained insight and tried some new behaviors (some consciously, and perhaps some unwittingly), and are actively chipping away at the thick layer of relationship habits that have encased you for so long.

One of the most consistent sources of confusion for my clients is bewilderment surrounding the notion of what *change* actually looks like. I am routinely asked, "But how do I actually change?" The confusion is understandable—change in its most minute form can't be observed, so how do we know whether it's actually happening? Consider the growth of a child: You can't physically see the child grow, but one day you suddenly realize that the child has gotten bigger. Though you couldn't note the actual changes as they occurred, you know that the child has been growing, and continues to grow, in the tiniest increments. Emotional growth works the same way—you can grow and mature without even realizing it while it's happening.

By this point, you, too, have grown and have begun to solidify your new, healthier approach to relationships. But don't be discouraged if this new perspective feels less than concrete right now, or even if you wonder whether you are changing in the right direction. Let's take a moment to think about the changes between seasons, and you will understand what I mean. Each winter, we slog through the cold until we encounter an occasional day of warm weather. Though the warmth often retreats and the cold may drift back in because the winter hasn't yet fully run its course, the hint that spring will soon come nevertheless remains.

At this point in your journey, you will start feeling your own intermittent hints of positive change—your reward for working to change something familiar and established. Yet just as a season arrives gradually and in fits and starts, emotional change, too, winds its way down a crooked path. Knowing just how unique and zigzagged the path can be toward the right relationship for you, I have focused these final chapters on factors that you should keep in mind as you make your way to your romantic future. In this chapter, we'll look at a few practical factors that will guide you toward a relationship where you can safely land.

The first part of this chapter was written for those of you who are looking to find a brand-new relationship, while the second half is for those of you who are in a relationship that is sorely in need of change.

Starting a New Relationship

Although the words can be spoken easily and strung together simply, the process involved in finding a better relationship—or, if you can imagine it, a really good one—tends to be much more difficult. So, I have boiled down your challenge to four guiding principles:

1. Be honest about what you need.
2. Prioritize emotional characteristics above all else.
3. Be realistic and flexible.
4. Be proactive.

You should feel encouraged to take a big-picture look at your love life, and to examine the partners you've chosen and why you have chosen them. I want to help you think about who you are, and who you would be most emotionally compatible with in a long-term relationship. (I could have written a book called *Ten Steps to Finding the Love of Your Life*, but I think that book—or something like it—has been written before.) When it comes to understanding the repetition of dysfunctional relationship patterns, we must go deeper to understand the problem and to force an identity shift so that you can approach relationships from a healthier perspective.

So far, I have purposely refrained from giving specific advice regarding how to find new dates, what to do on them, how to act, and so on. Should you try the online arena? Should you avoid it altogether? Questions such as these are best answered by a book or forum that focuses specifically on dating. My goal with this book is to help you stop repeating, help you create a healthier romantic identity, and then prime you for jumping back into the dating world—when you're ready.

However, I cannot do my job well without giving you some basic principles to keep in mind when you decide to seek out a new relationship. Keeping these principles in your back pocket will help you in that new relationship when it comes along, and will help to fortify the relationship and make it last. Let's take a look at each principle.

Be Honest about What You Need

The first part of this step seems simple enough: You must be honest with yourself about what your emotional needs are in a relationship. Here's the good news: you've already done much of the insight work to determine what those needs are. Flip back to the answers you provided for the inventories in Part III.

Peruse the inventories in Chapter 10 that focused on your personality, interests, and values and take a long, hard look at your responses. When you do this, let it be the kind of look you take in the mirror in the morning when you see yourself with bloodshot eyes and pillow creases on your face and think, "Wow, do I really look like that?" The reason you need to take such a raw and honest look at your real needs is so you can streamline your partner-selection process and look for someone sort of like . . . well, sort of like you. If you are going to make a relationship last longer than a few seasonal cycles, you must find someone who shares a fair number of your personality traits, values, and interests. While you are (I hope) not looking for your carbon copy (hint: if you are, then we need to talk more about narcissism), sharing core values and some interests will be necessary.

I always tell my clients that finding the partner with whom you are ultimately compatible will feel like finding a best friend to whom you're also attracted.

The honesty step also requires you to be open with yourself about what didn't work the last time, or the time before that, in your past relationships. Think about the traits and behaviors that deeply upset you and caused a great divide in your past relationships, and steer clear of these traits and behaviors as you seek out future partners. Specifically, go back through Chapter 11 and look at all of your responses as they relate to your old partners. Those responses will serve as fresh reminders of what to look for and what to avoid.

Remember when we talked about the differences between RRs and healthy lovers? One of the main differences is that healthy lovers avoid what didn't work in the past, while RRs tend to repeat those patterns without awareness or with the distorted expectation that *the next time will be different.* Save yourself some energy—the next time won't be different.

Take a few minutes and create a brief wish list of the traits you want your next partner to embody.

WISH LIST

Note in your Changes Journal:

- The three most important personality traits you want your next partner to have.
- A few behaviors you want him to engage in with you on a regular basis.
- A couple of examples of the types of compliment you would like him to give you.

Now that you have this brief wish list, I urge you to please use it. And I know that it goes without saying that for the most part, the compliments you should want from a man ought to center on your internal characteristics (your intelligence, kindness, sense of humor, and so on) rather than your external characteristics (physical attractiveness, sex appeal, etc.). Okay—just checking to make sure that you're already putting to use some of the lessons we've covered so far!

The second part of this step requires that you be honest with the new men you meet. Although you might be able to clearly articulate your needs to yourself, that internal insight won't get you too far if you don't express your needs clearly to someone you're dating. In fact, the beginning of a relationship is the most critical time to determine whether you and your prospective partner are going to be a good fit. In the past, you may have found yourself compulsively pulling a veil over parts of your personality or life for fear that a man might lose interest if he were to see all the facets. I have a simple answer to that concern: If he's not into it, good riddance! Let him know from the beginning who you are and what you need from a partner. If he's not going to be the partner you need, he can stick his thumb out and start hitchhiking for another woman. You can do your part by being honest, and that's all that you can control.

The discussion of honesty brings us to the next discussion: when to share your thoughts and needs. I've said that you should express your needs from the beginning, but how early is too early? Granted, your goal is not to be so direct with your new prospective partner that you come off too strong. After all, you're dating—not ordering a man off a menu at a restaurant. Successful dating requires finesse; you need to balance putting your needs out there with the sensitivity to know when to share personal information. Over the first month or so of a dating relationship, you can let your prospective partner know about what is important to you when it comes to a relationship. You're not supposed to achieve this goal by the end of date number one!

Prioritize Emotional Characteristics Above All Else

I hear you: Sexual attraction and sexual chemistry are important. That said, you *cannot* prioritize them over the emotional characteristics of your partner and the emotional chemistry you share—nothing about your relationship batting average is going to change if you don't take this truth to heart. Breaking the repetition cycle is about doing things differently the next time around, and that must include making the emotional characteristics of potential partners the number one priority as you look for a new a relationship. Obviously you'll be looking for someone with whom you are sexually and emotionally compatible, but let emotional compatibility be the top priority.

Be Realistic and Flexible

When a former clinical mentor of mine discussed the perils and dangers involved in falling in love, he would often sum up the subject by shaking his head and saying, "Dating is risky business." As you set out to find a partner—not just another boyfriend—do not get in your own way and set yourself up to fail. One of the most sure-fire ways to fail in your next relationship is to walk into it with unrealistic expectations. In fact, you'll remember that earlier in the book you learned that having unrealistic expectations is one of the main factors that cause RRs to repeat dysfunctional patterns.

Think about expectations for a moment from a slightly different angle: One difference between a child and an adult is that a child wants *everything*, while an adult knows she can't have everything. Keep in mind that it's both natural and inevitable that a future partner will frustrate you at times, and that he may engage in certain behaviors that make you want to pull your hair out—and not just a few hairs, but clumps at a time! Preparing for such realities will create more realistic expectations and help you to put things in perspective once you're knee-deep in the relationship. Here's an example of a healthy and realistic mix of positive and negative characteristics: "It drives me crazy that my partner's family is annoying and that he spends too much time watching sports on television, but he's a great listener, always respectful, and has a great sense of humor." You will find your own mix in your next relationship, but the goal is to accept an imperfect reality while also getting your most important emotional needs met in the relationship.

Be Proactive

It shouldn't come as news to you when I say that, overall, proactivity and an action-oriented approach go a long way toward solving relationship problems. Because we identified early on that you had a problem in the way you approached your past relationships, we proactively labeled the problem, reviewed its possible causes, and set out on a course to solve the problem. Remember to take a similar proactive approach to finding a new relationship.

It's not enough to simply put yourself out there and line up dates with new men—the process is a little more complex than that. You've learned that to break the repetition cycle and find a healthier relationship, you must first gain insight into your motivations, change some of your behaviors, and seek out environments where you will meet the kind of man with whom you're compatible. If, along the way, you find that you are coming up short in finding someone, what should you do?

Well, that's a new version of the same problem, so you must be proactive in solving it. In that case, you might need to change the locations in which you're socializing or perhaps make alterations to the social circle with whom you're spending time.

Also, put the word out on the street that you are interested in finding a partner. Remember the couples I asked you to interview about their relationships? Ask them to keep you in mind as they come across available men. Most important, when you make this proclamation to someone else, you hear yourself saying it, and the meaning of the words will become solidified in your mind. Remember not to tell anyone "I'm lonely," or "I really want a boyfriend." These admissions are dead-end streets. You don't want just anyone; you need an equal partner. One way that you can put the word out is to tell your friends, "Hey, if you come across someone who strikes you as solid and interesting, keep me in mind." Because everyone so easily gets caught up in the business of their own lives, they may need you to make an extra effort to remind them that they can be instrumental in connecting you with prospective partners.

Through constant vigilance and recalibration, you must determine what works best for you every step of the way. Perhaps at some point you'll need to take a break when you're feeling burned out from the pursuit. On the other hand, you may decide to ramp up the frequency of your dates, or opt to try online dating. Again, continually taking inventory will lead you to your relationship goal. Taken as a whole, the work you have been doing will help to confirm that you will use solid, adult judgment as you take on the challenge of finding a lasting partner. I am confident that your work will reward you!

Re-creating an Existing Relationship

If you are currently in a relationship that is not working, you must approach the problem in a solution-focused manner. It comes down to this: You need to decide whether it's best to stay or go. However, to avoid repeating, the cardinal rule is to make sure that your decision reflects the most balanced judgment and leads you to the happiest, most fulfilling relationship outcome in the long run. Here are five easy steps to help you determine whether you should end your relationship or make the effort to transform it into a better one—one that won't elicit in you constant frustration or suffering of any kind:

1. Identify your unmet needs.
2. Determine whether the problems can be fixed.
3. Create a Relationship Performance Improvement Plan.
4. Allow some time for change to occur.
5. Make your final decision.

These steps are clear and easy, so you should have no problem following them. Remember, the point is to simplify problems as much as possible and clear out the debris, leaving room for a streamlined path to resolution. Now let's discuss each of the five steps in detail.

IDENTIFY YOUR UNMET NEEDS

If you need a little help with this part, you can go back through your inventories, but you can probably come up with a list of your unmet needs fairly quickly, if not on the spot. Your unmet needs essentially are the problems in the relationship—what you want but are not getting. First, write down your unmet needs. You don't need a page-long list; you can probably sum up what you aren't getting in a few short words. Here's an example: 1) He is not meeting his end of the bargain in paying half of the bills because he's been unemployed for almost a year, 2) He never wants to do the same kinds of social things I want to do, 3) He never apologizes for things he does wrong or takes ownership for his faults, and 4) He regularly zones out when I'm talking or interrupts me. Your list, of course, will be unique to you, but you get the picture of the kind of unmet needs that can be listed here.

DETERMINE WHETHER THE PROBLEMS CAN BE FIXED

Frankly, this step merits its own book, but let me briefly describe how to tell the differences between the kinds of problems that are usually fixable and the kinds that are not. Basic personality traits (shyness, talkativeness, and so on) are fairly locked. As hard as someone could work in counseling or as much as someone could want to change these traits, they tend to be fairly consistent throughout one's life.

At the other end of the spectrum lie problems that are more easily fixed, which tend to be rooted in *behaviors* as opposed to ingrained traits. For example, coming home late without a previous phone call can easily be changed, as can verbal expressions of love and respect. When you look at the problems in your relationship and try to figure out whether they can change, you might get stuck at times or feel unable to judge a problem's level of fix-ability on your own. To get some objective feedback, create a focus group of about five people and ask them their opinions (in a general manner, if you prefer, without involving yourself or your partner in the question) about whether these are problems that are likely to change or not.

🔥 HOT COALS TASK: CREATE A RELATIONSHIP PERFORMANCE IMPROVEMENT PLAN

Before we go further, let me explain how I developed this intervention. In my administrative experiences as a program director at one particular mental health clinic, I was forced to learn the ins and outs of Human Resources. I learned about a valuable tool used to correct the problem behavior of an employee who is not meeting his job expectations by using a Performance Improvement Plan. This written document spells out which of the employee's behaviors must change and draws a time frame during which the change must occur—or else.

For this exercise, you are going to do something similar, and apply it to your own relationship. You are going to create your own *Relationship* Performance Improvement Plan. Once again, pull out your Changes Journal or simply grab some paper that you can hold on to for future reference. Write down the relationship problems that you identified in the first step, then cross out all of the items that you determined can't be changed in the second step. Next, document how you want each problem to be corrected and make a note of the time frame you will allow for the change to occur. The following is an example of what an RR's Relationship Performance Improvement Plan might look like, listing the problems and the corresponding changes required and their time frames.

PROBLEM

1. He loses his temper and yells at me.
2. We don't share any of the same interests, so we don't spend a lot of quality time together.
3. He is a terrible listener and never seems very interested in what's going on in my life.

REQUIRED CHANGE

1. When he's angry, he walks away or tells me calmly how he feels.
2. We need to start one new, shared activity that we engage in outside of the house at least once per week.
3. He will start asking me about my day, show interest in what I have to say, and listen to me when I talk to him about something that's important to me.

TIME FRAME

1. One month
2. Two weeks
3. One month

Notice that the plan focuses on specific problems—or, as specific as possible—and that the changes focus on behaviors. Now that you have an example of a Relationship Performance Improvement Plan, you can write your own and then move on to the next step.

ALLOW SOME TIME FOR CHANGE TO OCCUR

This step is pretty self-explanatory, so there's no need to dedicate too much time to it here. Problems aren't resolved overnight, so you need to be patient. Think about it: These problems took months or years to develop, so you can't expect them to disappear immediately. But the takeaway is that this is not a passive process. You are not simply staring out the window, waiting for things to change during the time that you specified on your Relationship Performance Improvement Plan. In fact, you should be working hard during that period. You should be looking for changes and noting them in your head or in your Changes Journal, as well as doing your part to help resolve the problem. If the problem is that your partner always comes home late without calling, it is important for you to not react emotionally. Instead, when he comes home, collect yourself and ask him to call you the next time he knows he'll be late. Explain to him why this is a problem (because it makes you feel disrespected, and so on), and ask him if he is willing to work on this behavior (getting him to verbally contract with you to change). At this point, you have tried and done all that you can do. He can choose to change or choose not to, but ultimately that choice is his. Remember that the choice he makes is one you must accept and not try to change for him. (Note: If the choice he makes is difficult for you to accept and you get stuck, go back to Chapter 13 and read and reread about mourning the loss. Your difficulty in accepting his decision might mean that you must learn to sit with the sadness you feel in order to move forward.)

MAKE YOUR FINAL DECISION

Once you have completed the Relationship Performance Improvement Plan and the time period has elapsed, it's judgment day. Either your needs are being met because you and your partner rose to the challenge and changed, or your needs continue to go unmet, forming a gaping hole that will only grow larger over time. One of the consistent reactions I see from clients at this point of the process is the tendency to act in a way that is best described as neurotic. For example, a given client may tell me, "He did change certain things, even though he didn't change a couple of the other things." These clients often focus on the silver lining rather than the major problems that have not been corrected. I always tell my clients that they have to be firm with themselves when it comes to their needs, and must force themselves to do so if necessary. This is no time to be wishy-washy. If there's a problem, try to fix it; however, if the problem persists, you must either accept it or move on.

By the end of this step, if you have decided to stay with your partner even if he has not met the goals of Relationship Performance Improvement Plan, understand that you have made a choice to settle and that you can no longer blame your partner for not meeting your needs. At that point, you have cosigned on your own unhappiness. But if you and your partner together met all of the goals of your plan, congratulations—you deserve the reward of your new, renovated relationship!

THE TAKEAWAY

You may have noticed that my tone changed a little in this chapter—more urgent, no-nonsense, and serious. The reason: You have done so much work up to this point to gain insight and change behaviors that you deserve a payoff—a better relationship. This chapter brings you one step closer toward that payoff. In this chapter, we focused on how to re-create your existing relationship or find a new one that's good for you, and each part had a fixed number of steps. The reason I emphasize simple steps is because they serve as boundaries, reminding you that you cannot afford to get wishy-washy or neurotic when it comes to your relationships. This chapter, like all of the others in this book, is all about identifying your needs and doing what needs to be done to see that they are met.

SELF-EVALUATION
Re-creating Your Love Life

1. For those of you who are single, take a look at your wish list. What is the most important item on your list?

2. For those of you who are in an existing relationship, which do you believe is the most difficult step in re-creating your relationship?

3. Forgetting your relationship status for a moment, what do you believe are the odds that you can transform an unhappy relationship into a good one? (Hint: Not a good chance unless *both* partners do an *awful* lot of work, and the problems are more behavioral than character-based!)

CHAPTER 18

Beware of Relationship Relapse

Avoid Triggers to Break the Habit

WE HAVE REVIEWED SOME guiding principles and practical behaviors you can use to find and cultivate a better, more fulfilling relationship, but the relationship toolbox would be incomplete if I did not introduce you to a challenge that you will likely face as you set out on your quest. In this chapter we'll take a look at what I can simply describe as the devil child of relationship repetition: relationship relapse. In this sense, relapse means reverting to the old bad patterns that always yielded the same negative result.

Before we excavate the gritty contents of relationship relapse, I need to put this concept in context for you. To do so, let's step back for a moment to discuss the field of addiction, including the treatments that have worked for so many in the past. As I have said throughout this book, my work with addicts has revealed to me just how many of the principles used to treat addiction apply remarkably well to the treatment of other problems, too. The repetition of dysfunctional relationship patterns is no exception. In treating addiction, specialists focus in part on relapse prevention, meaning that the goal is to prevent the addict from going back to his or her drug of choice in a vulnerable moment.

Think about your challenge from another perspective, as if you're doing everything you can to heal a broken bone. At the beginning of Chapter 13, you put on the cast. As you made your way through the last section on the book, you changed your behaviors as they relate to men, just as you would change your behaviors as a result of a broken bone. If it were a leg that you broke, for example, you'd stop walking on it! By this point in the healing process, the cast is ready to come off and your own broken approach to relationships is largely healed. However, you must remember at this point of the journey that you can't immediately believe that you're cured. In the same way that you wouldn't go run a half-marathon the day you get your cast off, you also shouldn't expect to jump right into a new, perfect relationship right away. As you go about your daily life, you must remember that this newly healed part of you is fragile. In this chapter, we're going to discuss what you need to do to avoid re-injury.

Certain triggers have been associated with relapse in addicts trying to recover from their addictions. These triggers include hunger, loneliness, anger, and fatigue. Armed with this knowledge, the specialists who treat addicts, as well as the addicts themselves, can prepare for such circumstances and do their best to protect themselves from the overwhelming power of their addiction. In other words, if we know that addicts are more likely to relapse in a moment when they are hungry, we can emphasize in their treatment the need for them to eat balanced meals and snacks throughout the day. In this way, the addict can do her best to prevent hunger from triggering a relapse into using her drug of choice.

Let's now consider the triggers unique to RRs. Of course, the specific triggers are going to vary according to your history, personality, and the type of pattern you repeated—and *notice I put that verb in the past tense,* because that behavior is indeed a thing of the past! As you go forward, you must know your triggers and come up with a plan to prevent your own relationship relapse. Though some differences will exist, there are a few common triggers that can ambush you all at once, jumping out of the bushes and hitting you at a hundred miles per hour. As you open yourself up to a new and better relationship you will find that you might relapse into your old ways unless you are careful to keep an eye on these triggers and block them as soon as your emotional radar picks up the signal that they lurk in the distance. There are clear strategies for coping with each trigger; these strategies have worked, not only with my clients, but with countless others the world over.

Relationship Relapse: Dangerous Triggers

- Ex Communication
- Encountering a "Ghost"
- Negative Feelings
- Dating or Falling in Love
- Big Event or Transition
- Alcohol or Drug Use

Let's review each so you can easily identify them, label them, and be prepared should they try to slither into your consciousness and coil themselves in the recesses of your mind.

Ex Communication

Breaking news: One of the most powerful triggers that can catapult you back to your old repeating ways is communication—contact of any kind—with an ex. Far too often, RRs who make an honest attempt at recovery make the fatal mistake of reaching out to or spending time with their exes. Sometimes, it's not even the most recent ex. These recovering RRs mistakenly tell themselves it's safe to reconnect with that old boyfriend because he's not the one they're heartsick over. Please remember this: While you are still recovering from repeating and haven't yet fully formed your new relationship identity, you need to be careful. Though there *will* come a day when you stand on solid romantic footing and would assuredly never settle for an unfulfilling partner or dysfunctional romantic situation, you might not have fully created that new relationship identity quite yet. Until you reach that point, it can be *highly dangerous* to communicate with any exes. The reason: your exes remind you of who you used to be, not who you are changing into, and being around these people can cause you to interact with them in the ways you did in the past.

Coping Strategy: As a rule, avoid contact with an ex until you feel sturdy and no longer feel drawn to men with the emotional and/or physical characteristics he possesses. Do not mislead yourself: there is no timeline for this process, as it could take months for some or years for others. Know yourself and your limits and *please* honor them!

Encountering a "Ghost"

Obviously, there is no actual ghost with a rattling chain; we're talking metaphorically about a romantic ghost, meaning someone who reminds you of the type of man you used to be attracted to. No matter what your pattern, you will likely be triggered by various types of men. In fact, feeling triggered might be confusing, so much so that you may not even know what's happening or that you're getting triggered at all.

The truth is that there are going to be certain traits that will remind you of your old type of man, and you will occasionally find these traits along your dating journey in men you've never met before. As you wade through dating waters and find yourself in new situations with unfamiliar men, be vigilant about your feelings and the tone of the interaction. Most of all, check yourself when you feel overwhelming lust or attraction. Given your history of repetition, odds are that a man who triggers this kind of powerful reaction is reminiscent of your old type. In these instances, the best way to be a friend to yourself will be to turn on your heel and head in the opposite direction.

Coping Strategy: Take a time-out by physically removing your-self from the situation, calling your relationship sponsor or a friend, and seeking out a quiet environment that will allow you to sit with and hear your own feelings. When you take a step back and calm your mind, your judgment improves and you can make better decisions—decisions that aren't related to immediate gratification but rather to what is best for your future.

Negative Feelings

Sadness, anger, hopelessness, and other negative feelings can act like mind-altering substances, seductively propelling you to regress to your old ways. Few triggers are as powerful when it comes to guiding you into the arms of someone who is not good for you. These feelings can make you feel alone and vulnerable, and that little voice in the back of your head can start sending you some not-so-good messages. All of a sudden, the new guy who at first seemed arrogant starts seeming likable and misunderstood, while another one who told you he has a history of cheating with past girlfriends suddenly seems less repugnant and more attractive as you give him credit for being so honest with you. Before you know it, you might start feeling wishy-washy and feel torn about changing. In these moments, you might tell yourself that you can't change who you're attracted to and, as a result, give yourself permission to go back to the same kind of man with whom you shared past failed relationships.

Coping Strategy: This strategy has two parts. First, come up with a mantra that works for you and repeat it in your head several times. For example, you might want to say something to yourself such as, "It's not what a man says that counts, but what he does." Second, when negative feelings threaten to drop anchor and settle in, immediately make plans to switch into an activity that improves your mood and distracts you from the negativity. For example, this might include putting on your running shoes and going for a quick walk or run, or perhaps calling a friend who makes you laugh.

Dating or Falling in Love

Nothing can stir up a mess of feelings as swiftly as falling for someone new. There often comes a point in a new relationship when the recovering RR begins to realize that intimacy is mounting and feelings are becoming more intense. What, if you were to guess, often happens next for the RR? Quite simply, intimacy fears pop up like soldiers jumping out of a bunker, and defense mechanisms rush onto the scene, impelling you to guard yourself against your developing feelings. It's not uncommon for avoidance ("Oh, maybe I'll see him next week instead of this week") or rationalization ("I'm not calling him because it probably wouldn't work out with him anyway") to kick in.

Coping Strategy: When intimacy sets off your alarms and you start to feel uncomfortable, sit with your feelings rather than act them out. In these moments, avoid making *any* decisions about the relationship, and find a healthy outlet for your anxiety.

Big Event or Transition

It doesn't take a clinical psychologist to understand how a major negative (or even positive) life event can trigger a person to regress and engage in behavior that emphasizes immediate gratification over long-term fulfillment. When that negative behavior is repeating a toxic relationship pattern, it makes sense that you could feel triggered by a major event or transition to go back to an ex or seek out a new man who has the same characteristics that doomed your past relationships. For example, if you start a new job and get home at the end of the first day feeling lonely and frustrated, you might long for emotional or physical affection and start flipping through your little black book to find someone to comfort you. Yet it isn't only negative events that can lead to relationship relapse. In fact, occasions that foster happy emotions or excitement—weddings, parties, and other events—can trigger relapse. When you are triggered, your body can sometimes feel as if it is on a sort of high, and such body stimulation can cloud your thinking and better judgment. This can have bad consequences if your behaviors lead you to a man who is not ultimately good for you.

Coping Strategy: If you are at home or near home when you are triggered by a negative event, use some of the old standbys to ground you: exercise, talking about your feelings with someone you trust, and engaging in other healthy behaviors that comfort you. Those may include cooking something delicious, lighting some candles, and curling up with a book that truly engages you and captivates your attention. If you're away from home and an event—say, a wedding—is triggering you, remove yourself from the environment for five or ten minutes, take ten or so deep breaths, and text message yourself some comforting thoughts to remind yourself that this moment will pass. It never fails: These happy or upsetting moments are powerful precursors to calling an ex or seeking out someone new just to feel better in that moment, so you must use good coping strategies to make sure that you don't fall into this predictable trap.

Alcohol or Drug Use

You may believe that substance use is a factor so self-evident that we don't need to cover it, but the reality is that drinking or using other drugs is one of the most common types of self-medicating and, most important for our purposes, is one of the most powerful triggers that will thrust you back into dysfunctional relationship patterns. The relationship between using substances and regressing to your old ways is simple: the very thing you turn to (drugs or alcohol) to dull your negative feelings simultaneously clouds your judgment and causes you to engage in behaviors that cause even more anxiety in the end.

In other words, using alcohol or drugs is going to confuse how you feel, cause you to think irrationally, and propel you to engage in behavior that is based on immediate gratification as opposed to long-term gain. One of the surest ways to undo everything you've worked hard to break free from is to self-medicate with substances. Understand that alcohol or drug use is going to seriously increase your risk of returning to an ex or seeking out a new man who reminds you of an ex. Don't forget that the point of this book is to move away from that old dysfunctional identity so you can incarnate a new, healthier identity—one that is drawn to men you're compatible with! In short, avoiding alcohol and drugs will make it easier for you to avoid relapsing into your old dysfunctional relationship patterns.

Coping Strategy: Be careful when it comes to substances. I could tell you to refrain from using substances altogether, but sometimes telling a recovering person "no" actually causes them to act out even more. The point is to protect yourself. If you are going to drink alcohol, for example, limit the amount and be wary of emotionally or sexually connecting with anyone while you are under the influence. If you drink when you go out socially, you might consider making it a rule that you can give a man your number but you won't engage in any sexual behavior with him—not even kissing. The truth is that any physical behavior you share with a man can bond you to him emotionally, and you need to sober up before you can determine whether he is worth your time and energy.

Quick Tips to Ward Off Relationship Relapse

1. *Slow Down:* Because you're more likely to relapse and move toward a man who is not good for you when you are feeling unbalanced or are moving through your own life too quickly, it is imperative that you slow down and collect yourself. In your romantic life, you must feel grounded in order to use sound judgment.

2. *Nourish Yourself:* Eat balanced meals and snack on healthy foods throughout the day. A balanced nutrition plan will help keep your mood stable and will make you less prone to feeling lethargic or anxious and turning to a man for a quick emotional pick-me-up.

3. *Use Your Sponsor and Journal:* Please do not underestimate the importance of this relapse prevention tool. As we discussed earlier, you must elect a sponsor and you must use that sponsor consistently. In addition, writing in a journal, a notebook you keep in a kitchen drawer, or whatever paper you can find will help you to sort out and organize your thoughts and feelings so that you can make good decisions and engage in positive, productive behaviors when it comes to men. Ideally, you have found that using your Changes Journal throughout this book has provided proof that writing about how you feel can not only lift your feelings, but also help you figure out what it is that you're feeling in the first place!

4. *Monitor Your Four Burners:* If you take only a few lessons from this book, I hope that the four-burner theory, which we discussed in Chapter 16, is one of them. To quickly review, this concept says that too often we overfocus on one particular area of our lives—often our romantic relationship, but it could also be work or something else—to the exclusion of the other areas that need attention. Finding and holding on to a healthy relationship calls for a balanced approach to your life and realistic expectations, and it requires that each partner be a functional and productive person on his or her own. For this reason, you must look at the major areas of your life—the four burners—and make sure that something positive is cooking on each burner. In the end, you are much less likely to relapse back into the repeated patterns if you make sure all of the various areas of your life are in working order.

5. *Use Chapter 19 Like It's a Breath of Fresh Air:* In the next (and final) chapter, you'll find some basic behaviors that will help to keep you grounded and which have the added benefit of preventing relationship relapse. In the chapter, I describe fundamental ways to soothe yourself, which you will soon discover is the secret foundation to finding true, lasting love.

THE TAKEAWAY

In this chapter, we covered the slippery slope of relationship relapse. Briefly, this refers to falling back into your old dysfunctional relationship pattern by spending time with a man—either a new one or an ex—who is not good for you. I highlighted dangerous triggers that can lead to relationship relapse, and paired each with a coping strategy you can use to help you fight off relapse. Finally, I introduced you to coping strategies, which are quick tips—sort of like guiding principles—to help you plant your feet firmly on the ground so that you are less vulnerable to relapsing in weak or vulnerable moments. As we begin the last chapter, you can look forward to learning about some final tools and exercises that can help you enrich your relationships—and the rest of your life, as well.

SELF-EVALUATION

Recognizing and Deflecting a Rebound

1. What would your romantic ghost look like—the one that could most powerfully trigger you?

2. What is an example of a negative life event—one that is realistic, given your life circumstances—that could make you vulnerable to relapsing with a man who isn't good for you?

3. Which of the coping strategies do you imagine you will use the most frequently in the future?

CHAPTER 19

Self-Solace

How It's Related to True Love

WELL, YOU'VE DONE IT—YOU'VE arrived at the final chapter. Since starting out with my prescription for change, you have come a long way in changing the way you operate romantically. But before I cast you off on your own to actually bring a healthier relationship to life, I want to leave you with some basic tools that will help you in your relationship search, in a future relationship, and in your life overall. Your metaphorical broken bone is largely healed, but it's important to incorporate some light "physical therapy" into your life to encourage it to heal as solidly as it possibly can.

Giving up the repeating reflex and wearing a new, healthy relationship identity will require much greater attention to your needs and general life circumstances. By now you have learned the most important lesson: You must avoid a one-track focus on your romantic relationships—even once you've found a really healthy one. Part of its health depends on the idea that you will not rely solely on the relationship to fulfill you. Remember: The quality of the rest of your life—and how much you invest in it and cultivate it—has everything to do with the quality of your love life. Moving on, the final step in our journey together is to review the concept of self-solace, which I am confident will help you in ways you can't yet predict.

What Is Self-Solace?

You may have heard of the term "self-soothing" before—it refers to your ability to make yourself feel better without outside help. Healthy self-soothing implies that you don't need someone else to make you feel better, you don't need alcohol or drugs to take you out of your feelings, and you don't need to act out in destructive or self-destructive ways because you can't tolerate whatever thoughts and feelings you may have in a given moment. The ability to self-soothe means you have the ability to simultaneously face negative situations and still manage to restore your own inner balance by treating yourself well and managing your feelings until they pass. Self-solace reflects the state in which you are able to calm yourself and keep yourself feeling safe and good no matter what is going on around you.

Why You Need to Self-Soothe

Now is an excellent time to practice self-soothing and to familiarize yourself with this type of coping. Why now, you ask? If I had to choose one event that has the potential to detonate a trunk full of raw anxieties and feelings, dating and looking for a new partner would sit at the very top of my list. Building these self-soothing behaviors into your daily or weekly routine will serve the following purposes. It will:

- Remind you that you know how to make yourself feel good and treat yourself well
- Create balance in your daily life so you don't overly depend on a relationship or man
- Make you feel whole and solid, meaning you'll make a better, more complete 50 percent of a future romantic union

In addition, there are benefits of self-soothing that you can take advantage of in your new relationship. In this way, self-soothing isn't necessarily a purely solitary pursuit, and it bears fruits you can share in a healthy relationship. Self-soothing can benefit your future relationship in the following ways. It will:

- Provide you with pleasurable activities that you can share and enjoy with your partner
- Introduce new behaviors to your partner that he may not have tried before or may not even have known he would enjoy
- Create intimacy with your partner that is based on a mutual appreciation of activities, providing you with a foundation that you can share now and in the future

Self-Soothing Is a Lifestyle, Not a Fad Diet

As crucial as self-soothing activities and outlets are, they often get lost in the chaos of everyday life. As a therapist, I am regularly confronted with the challenges of finding and maintaining self-soothing behaviors in my clients' daily lives. I see countless clients who begin to engage in a given healthy activity but soon leave it behind, tossing it aside like a no-longer-useful paper plate. These individuals tell me that they engaged in the new, healthy activities for a period of time but later gave them up for any number of reasons. I tell all of my clients that maintaining healthy outlets—nourishing activities that ground you—is necessary, *not* optional.

Self-Soothing Outlets

There are several valuable self-soothing behaviors that can serve as important outlets in your weekly routines, grounding you and providing a solid foundation for your future relationship and for your life overall. Let's review each outlet to start to understand how they nourish you and keep you balanced. You'll see that each outlet includes brief background information about that specific behavior, an explanation of how the behavior soothes you, examples of ways you can practice the behavior, and a description of how practicing this behavior can positively impact your future romantic relationship.

Soother: Water

Think about the way a human life begins: It all starts with water. Wrapped in the womb, the fetus is nurtured and nourished in water, a safe refuge from the perils and challenges of the world for which the growing infant is not yet ready. Later in life, incorporating a water outlet into your life will help soothe you, restore your inner balance, and reach a state of momentary peace.

HOW IT SOOTHES

Unlike other soothing activities, being submerged in water creates a direct sensation on your skin and immediately stimulates your senses. Stimulating the senses is important because it positively transforms your mood and mindset, directing the focus from your brain (the center of your thoughts and feelings) to your body (in this case, the sensation of water on the skin).

WAYS TO ENJOY WATER

Taking baths; recreational or athletic swimming; relaxing in a pool; walking along the water's edge; or even sitting with a good book or your journal by a river, pond, or lake.

WHEN TO USE IT

When you need to calm yourself after a day at work, when you are nervous or worried, and to maintain your calm when you're already feeling good and balanced.

RELATIONSHIP APPLICATION

Incorporating a water soother into your regular routines will help keep you calm and grounded regardless of the stage of your journey— whether you're looking for a relationship or maintaining a good one once you've found it. The healthier you are mentally, the more likely you are to attract a healthy partner. Water outlets help keep you balanced and grounded in an (at times) insane world. In addition, this self-soothing outlet provides you with a wonderful coping mechanism during the inevitable times of difficulty in a relationship.

Soother: Food

Please note that I am *not* presenting food as a comforter in the way you may be imagining—plates of mashed potatoes and other carbohydrates to drown out your feelings when you're feeling anxious or down. I am presenting food here as a soother in a way that involves the appreciation of food by means of greater awareness and consciousness of its nourishing and comforting value. What makes a certain food behavior an actual nourishing outlet is the amount of thought that goes into it and the degree of nourishment you derive from it.

HOW IT SOOTHES

Healthy food provides you with fuel and makes you feel good. Most important, incorporating a food outlet requires you to slow down and to be conscious of what you prepare, cook, or put into your body. Also, food stimulates your senses—taste, smell, sight, and touch. When you stimulate your senses, you nourish yourself and come out of your own mind a little bit. In other words, this nourishing behavior transports your senses to a different experience and, in turn, brings you to a better state of mind. This behavior can be especially soothing if the mood or thoughts you are engulfed in are upsetting ones.

WAYS TO ENJOY FOOD

Cooking on Saturday or Sunday (when you likely have more time); preparing food or cooking when you're home alone; watching cooking shows or reading recipes and then trying them yourself; starting a rotating dinner party with a group of friends; taking a cooking class; creating a special meal time once or twice per week during which you try new foods, spices, or cuisines; having a weekly picnic; or making a regular trip to a farmer's market.

RELATIONSHIP APPLICATION

Building a food outlet into your weekly routine reminds you that you know what your body needs, that you can meet your own needs, and that you make a conscious effort to treat yourself well. Again, stimulating your senses with food helps you to come out of your mind in a positive way. This is helpful when you have a history of bad relationships that may have consumed your thoughts and drained too much mental energy. Once you are in a healthy relationship, sharing a food outlet can provide one of the most intimate experiences you can have with a partner, whether cooking for him, cooking together, or visiting restaurants or regions that specialize in your favorite foods.

Soother: Breathing

Breathing as a soothing behavior refers to disciplined breathing, a predictable pattern of breathing in which you must concentrate on regulating your breath. This allows you to mentally take a step back from your circumstances and focus on the bigger picture. When it comes to making decisions and deciding how you feel, an awareness of the bigger picture will vastly improve your judgment and, in turn, your decisions as well. In engaging in this self-soother, you will find that you learn the art of positively directing and focusing your mind.

HOW IT SOOTHES

A breathing outlet can reduce anxiety, depressed feelings, or anger when you feel that things are overwhelming or out of control.

WAYS TO GET BREATHING

Calm breathing outlets include meditation, yoga, peaceful walks, and gardening; highly active breathing outlets include jogging, dance, kickboxing, and hiking.

RELATIONSHIP APPLICATION

Incorporating disciplined breathing outlets into your weekly routine has a major positive impact on your energy level and mood. When you meet a man, or once you are in a relationship, having good breathing outlets keeps your mood happy, your mind balanced, and your focus on your mind and body as opposed to overly focusing on your partner (what he's thinking or feeling) or worrying about the current state or the future of your relationship once you're in it.

Soother: Touch

Touching and being touched bear extraordinary healing powers, providing a necessary part of feeling good and balanced.

HOW IT SOOTHES

Being touched is the ultimate comforter, and touching someone else and making him or her feel good makes you feel good, too. Touching and sharing touch fosters a sense of warmth in you and the person with whom you share touch. Simply put, touch just feels good.

WAYS TO ENJOY TOUCH

Exchanging hugs or kisses as a regular social gesture; holding hands or rubbing one's back while walking or talking; moisturizing your body or specific body parts; sharing foot or hand massages with a friend while watching your favorite television show; getting a regular massage, manicure, or pedicure.

RELATIONSHIP APPLICATION

Incorporating regular touching outlets into your daily routine will make you feel good and balanced and make your mood lighter and more positive. The more often you can reach and maintain this positive mood and outlook, the more attractive you will be to future partners and the more balanced you will feel as you call upon your own judgment to determine which partners are worth your time. Once you are in a relationship, building regular touch into your relationship—touch that does not revolve around sex or the pursuit of it—will increase intimacy and help you and your partner see each other as safe harbors.

Soother: Pets

Volumes of research suggests that taking care of a pet is good for your mental health, and being responsible for a pet can teach you important life lessons and help you mature emotionally. If I could recommend just one factor to add to your life—something to get cooking on one of your life burners—it would be to take care of a pet. Few relationships are as healing and inspiring as having a pet to love and take care of. It's important to note that a pet outlet isn't limited to animals (keep reading and you'll see what I mean).

HOW IT SOOTHES

If you have a pet animal, petting your animal not only relaxes your pet—it relaxes you as well. In addition, petting the animal creates an intimate moment that includes giving and receiving love, an exchange that is soothing and warm.

WAYS TO ENJOY PETS

With actual pets: petting or playing with your pet; feeding and supplying your pet with water; monitoring and taking care of any medical needs, and so forth; with nonanimal "pets": taking care of plants, including watering, trimming, and monitoring your plants' growth.

RELATIONSHIP APPLICATION

Taking care of a pet helps you learn how to develop intimacy in a relationship, because care of a pet brings with it many of the same feelings that come with an intimate human relationship—dependence, love, and even frustration. When you have a pet, whether animal or plant, you become accustomed to taking good care of something else, which serves as an important reminder that you, too, need good, nourishing care and regular emotional feeding.

Soother: Compliments

Giving compliments is not a false, put-on way of currying favor from others, but rather a conscious effort to think about the feelings of others, treat others well, and open yourself up to intimate exchanges with others. Incorporating compliments into your repertoire is based on feeling comfortable with expressing warm feelings to others, and looking for the good in people rather than highlighting the negative. The goal is to rise above the acknowledgment of simple external characteristics (such as, "You look nice") in favor of the more meaningful internal characteristics of a person (such as, "You are sweet to so often offer help to others when they need it").

HOW IT SOOTHES

Making someone else feel good simply makes you feel good. When you compliment someone, you can see the physical changes in that individual's face and body: their features soften and often transform into a smile, and you can see their shoulders relax. Inducing and witnessing this effect has a positive effect on your own feelings and mood, in turn. Such intimate exchanges can take you out of your previous mental mindset (for instance, if you were worried about a work project or some other daily challenge) and allow for an emotional glow in which the two of you can feel warm and engaged with each other.

WAYS TO GIVE COMPLIMENTS

Verbally commenting on the positive characteristics of friends, family, and coworkers, and graduating to complimenting others you don't know as well; writing someone a note of appreciation; doing something special for someone even if you don't owe them a specific favor (for example: cooking or baking something, taking someone to lunch, or purchasing tickets for that person to a special event).

RELATIONSHIP APPLICATION

Incorporating regular compliments into your daily routines reminds those around you that you appreciate them. Complimenting others allows for an intimate exchange between two people, as each lets the other past the rigid wall of politeness into the more intimate corners of a more genuine and spontaneous emotional moment. In broader terms, feeling comfortable giving compliments shows that you are able to acknowledge the positive traits and behaviors in others, and to show appreciation and respect for them. Knowing how to respect and acknowledge others sets the stage for you to be able to more easily recognize it when someone treats you well and shows you kindness. If you truly know what love and respect feels like from others, you'll be less likely to accept anything less than that from men. Further, once you're in a healthy relationship, appreciating the positive and routinely complimenting and thanking your partner provides long-lasting fuel that fortifies any relationship. In other words, if you and your partner know how to appreciate and compliment each other, you'll simply like each other more in the long run.

Soother: Spiritual, Nondenominational, or Religious Prayer

There are many ways that you can engage in prayer—whether it be religious, spiritual, or nondenominational. My intention is not to endorse a particular religious affiliation but to present prayer in a universal context: as a disciplined, thoughtful activity in which you focus on what you appreciate, love, and want for the future. Prayer in whichever way you practice it can enrich your daily life, connecting you with something bigger than yourself and your own specific life circumstances. Incorporating prayer into your daily routines is a nourishing behavior, one that makes you feel good and provides you with something else cooking on another burner of your life.

HOW IT SOOTHES

Prayer helps to organize the chaos of the day, reminding you that you have things to be thankful for and giving you a sense of the bigger picture beyond your thoughts and feelings in that immediate moment. A simple prayer brings immediate relief but also bears a longer-term purpose: By removing the focus on the specific circumstances and difficulties in your life, you gain a sense of the bigger picture and world within which you live. Such a transformation can provide relief from anxiety, stress, and overwhelming feelings.

WAYS TO INTEGRATE PRAYER

Morning, afternoon, or evening prayer prior to or following sleep or a nap when you take a moment to say "thank you" for what you have; writing in a gratitude journal; asking God or the higher power you believe in for help and wisdom when it comes to a particular problem or a larger life goal.

RELATIONSHIP APPLICATION

Regularly engaging in a prayer outlet has an indirect effect on your romantic relationship. Relying on a higher power and counting your blessings can help you to keep things in perspective when you hit a rough patch in your relationship, and allow you to give thanks for the good in your partner rather than overfocus on the negative.

Self-Solace Comes with Lifelong Benefits

Building self-soothing behaviors into your daily routines has several benefits. Most important, these behaviors allow you to make yourself feel good and balanced, and provide you with crucial coping mechanisms you can use when faced with situations, thoughts, or feelings that are difficult or uncomfortable. This foundation, of course, yields a secondary gain: It sets the stage for you to attract healthy partners and to help you maintain a healthy relationship once you've found one. True self-solace requires you to incorporate a lifestyle change; it is not a trend like a fad diet you try for a month but later give up. In other words, building these outlets into your lifestyle means that they're a regular, constant component, not behaviors you happen to engage in *if you feel like it.* Too often clients in my office will say, "Well, I didn't do [insert healthy outlet] the past few weeks because . . ." Bottom line: If you live by the lifestyle code as opposed to the diet code, you cannot succumb to irresponsibility and let yourself miss a few weeks of a behavior that soothes and grounds you. Ultimately, these behaviors—those that make you feel more alive, balanced, and whole—are non-negotiable. Finally, you probably noticed that the self-soothers all share something in common: They employ life's most basic elements—water, food, touch, and so on. These elements are the ones that truly make you feel nurtured and balanced. Ultimately, you'll find that a balanced mental state—deriving from your ability to use these self-soothers—allows you to use your best judgment and insight as you sift through future potential partners and decide which one deserves your time and energy.

THE TAKEAWAY

In this chapter, we bypassed the expressway and took the scenic route, extending our focus beyond your relationships to look at the bigger picture: building self-soothing behaviors into your life so that you become wiser and more balanced, the ultimate foundation for a romantic partnership to come. You learned how to love yourself and reviewed valuable self-soothers to incorporate into your daily routines. These behaviors function as nourishing outlets that make you feel good and remind you that you don't need to depend on a man—or anyone else, for that matter—to make you feel whole and complete. When you are ready to step back into the romantic ring, you will find that the healthier you are, the more likely you are to attract healthy partners.

SELF-EVALUATION
Treating Yourself with Kindness

1. What is self-solace? Why is it important?

2. Which of the outlets, if any, do you already practice? Which of the outlets do you least believe in or least want to try? (Hint: This is the outlet you most need to try.)

3. Why might the discussion about soothing prayer remind you of self-talk, the running inner dialogue we talked about earlier in the book? (Hint: They're siblings.)

A Few Final Words

Keep the Momentum Going

THERE'S SOMETHING SWEET ABOUT taking on a new challenge and later getting the first glimmers of progress toward your goal. After staring your romantic demons straight in the face, chapter by chapter, I hope that you have begun to sense real progress toward your own goal—knocking the wind out of romantic repetition so that this behavior never haunts you again. Now that we've come to the end of our journey together, you might be wondering to yourself, what's next?

It goes without saying that having a book to guide you through your recovery process makes the direction you're headed in easier to see, yet what follows will require that you step up to the plate in a new and different way. How you proceed from here, including the romantic decisions that you make from this point forward, is entirely up to you. Hopefully, I've helped you gain the insight you need and provided not only the tools that will help you find your right match, but also the tools you will need to stay strong and quiet your fears and anxieties. Don't forget that the ultimate goal isn't simply to find a relationship, but rather to find one that helps you to flourish. Remember that one of the most important lessons of this book is that struggling in a dead-end relationship depletes your energy and wastes your time. This is important, because I'm sure that you've got better things that you could be doing with your time, and I believe you were born to flourish!

I know that struggling in relationships and questioning whether a good one truly awaits can be a frustrating and lonely experience. My purpose in writing this book has been not to highlight the negative but instead to emphasize how truly *possible* change is. When you hit a romantic roadblock and feel like giving up or reverting back to your old relationship ways, pull out this book again and go through the Insight Inventories and do some—or all—of the exercises again. Using this book as an ongoing resource, rather than as a one-time read, will ensure that you keep the momentum going. Though there's no telling when a better partner will appear, trust that knowing yourself and your needs better will direct you to a partner with whom you are more compatible than the partners in your past.

As this chapter of your life comes to a close, you should feel extremely proud of yourself for confronting your relationship issues and honestly trying to elevate your relationships and your life for the better. At this point in your recovery process, you are perched at a crossroads of sorts: You're not fully recovered yet, but you're not repeating, either. At this fork in the road, you can rewrite your relationship script for the future.

Most of all, I want you to trust that you were not born to have an adult life that is anguish-filled, one where the best you can get is less-than-love and some bombed-out version of settling. Continue to do the work and cultivate yourself, and you will find that you will never again repeat the dysfunctional patterns of the past. As a mentor of mine once said, "Every step you take away from someone who isn't good for you is one step closer to someone who is."

Regardless of which pattern you repeated in the past, the script of your love life in the future is a blank slate. Take solace in the fact that you have already kick-started the process of creating a new identity, one that is wiser and more cautious about whom you let into your life and your heart. I am confident that with continued consciousness and effort, you will find, like an architect at work at her drafting table, that you can—and will—design the relationship you've always wanted.

Bibliography

Beck, Judith S. *Cognitive Therapy: Basics and Beyond. New York: Guilford Press, 1995.*

Murray, H. A. *Explorations in Personality.* New York: Oxford University Press, 1938.

Overmier, J. Bruce, and Martin E. P. Seligman. "Effects of Inescapable Shock Upon Subsequent Escape and Avoidance Responding." *Journal of Comparative and Physiological Psychology* 63(1): 28–33 (1967).

Pennebaker, James W., and Janel D. Seagal. "Forming a Story: The Health Benefits of Narrative." *Journal of Clinical Psychology* 55(10): 1243–1254 (1999).

Index

About the Authors

Dr. Seth Meyers

Dr. Seth is a licensed clinical psychologist in private practice in Los Angeles who also works with the Los Angeles County Department of Mental Health. He regularly appears on television and radio, and contributes to many national magazines and newspapers on relationship and other clinical issues. He is a blogger for *Psychology Today* and writes his own blog on relationship issues at *www.DrSeth.blogspot.com*. You can learn more about him, his phone consultations, and his seminars across the United States at his official website: *www.DrSethRelationshipExpert.com*.

Katie Gilbert

Katie Gilbert is a freelance writer and editor whose writing has been published regularly in *Psychology Today, Institutional Investor*, and *Willamette Week*, an alternative newsweekly in Portland, Oregon. She is also a senior editor with David Lombardino & Associates Editing and Proofreading Services.